D0074819

Soviet Society Today

Soviet Society Today

Michael Rywkin

M. E. Sharpe, Inc.
ARMONK, NEW YORK
LONDON, ENGLAND

Available in the United Kingdom and Europe from M. E. Sharpe,
Publishers, 3 Henrietta Street, London WC2E 8LU.

Design by Sonja Godfried.

On the title page: "Glory to the Great Soviet People." Photograph
by the author.

"Voices" are translated by the author or excerpted from the translation
journals *Soviet Law and Government* and *Soviet Sociology*, published by
M. E. Sharpe, Inc. by arrangement with VAAP, the Soviet copyright
agency.

Library of Congress Cataloging-in-Publication Data

Rywkin, Michael.
    Soviet society today / by Michael Rywkin.

    p.   cm.
    Bibliography: p.
    Includes index.
    ISBN 0-87332-444-7 : ISBN 0-87332-445-5 (pbk.) :
      1. Soviet Union—Social conditions—1970-   2. Soviet Union—
Politics and government—1982-   I. Title.
HN523.5.R98 1989
306'.0947—dc19   89-4192
                                                    CIP

Printed in the United States of America

To the memory of my father—
my first teacher about Soviet society

Contents

The Standard of Living

The Way of Life

Uniformity and Diversity

Postscript

Chronology

1861	Abolition of serfdom
1904–05	Russo–Japanese War
1905	First Russian Revolution
1906–10	Stolypin reforms in agriculture
1914–18	World War I
1917	February (March) Revolution
	October (November) Revolution
	Secret police force (Cheka) established
1918–20	Civil War (Red Army vs. White Armies)
1918–26	"Basmachi" revolt in Central Asia
1921–27	Lenin's New Economic Policy
1924	Death of Lenin
1924	First federal Constitution of the USSR
1926–29	Stalin defeats rivals, consolidates power
1928	Beginning of First Five-year Plan
	Collectivization of agriculture begins
1929	Mass deportation of "kulaks" begins
1932	Internal passport system reintroduced
1933	Beginning of Second Five-year Plan
1933–38	Mass purges and deportations
1934	"Socialist realism" made official doctrine
1935	"Stakhanovite" movement begins
1936	"Stalin Constitution"
1939	Nazi–Soviet Nonaggression Pact
	Partition of Poland
	Annexation of Bessarabia, Estonia, Latvia, Lithuania
1939–40	Russo–Finnish War

1941	Germany invades USSR
1944	Deportation of "punished nationalities"
1945	Allied victory over Germany and Japan
1946	Beginning of "Cold War"
1949–50	Collectivization of agriculture in annexed territories
1950	Korean War begins
1952	The "doctors' plot"
1953	Death of Stalin
	Nikita Khrushchev becomes Party First Secretary
1956	Khrushchev's "secret speech" denouncing Stalin
1957	Soviet Sputnik launched
1960	Sino–Soviet break
1964	Leonid Brezhnev replaces Khrushchev
1974	Alexander Solzhenitsyn expelled from the USSR
1977	"Brezhnev Constitution"
1979	High point of Jewish and German emigration
1979	Soviet intervention in Afghanistan
1980	Andrei Sakharov exiled to Gorky
1982	Death of Leonid Brezhnev
	Yuri Andropov becomes General Secretary
1984	Death of Yuri Andropov
	Konstantin Chernenko becomes General Secretary
1985	Death of Konstantin Chernenko
	Mikhail Gorbachev becomes General Secretary
1985	Beginning of "perestroika" campaign
1985–88	"Rehabilitation" of victims of Stalinism
	Anti-alcohol campaign
1986	April nuclear plant disaster at Chernobyl
1986	December riots in Alma-Alta
1987–88	Armenian–Azerbaijani clashes in Nagorno-Karabakh
	Demands for greater autonomy in Baltic republics
	Introduction of "family contracts" in agriculture
	Spread of co-operative movement
1988	Soviet troop withdrawal from Afghanistan begins
	December earthquake in Soviet Armenia
1989	Election of Congress of People's Deputies

Acknowledgments

The material for this book comes from years of study of Soviet reality through research, teaching, professional contacts, travel, and personal experience.

In 1984, and again in 1987, I was given the opportunity to travel to the USSR under the sponsorship of IREX, The International Research and Exchanges Board. The research for this book was supported in part by a grant from IREX, with funds provided by the National Endowment for the Humanities and the United States Information Agency. None of these organizations is responsible for the views expressed here.

The City College of New York facilitated my task by granting me a sabbatical leave in 1987–88, and Columbia University libraries gave me access to their excellent collections. No other institutional funding has been secured, a testimony to the author's low degree of grantsmanship expertise.

This book could not have been completed in its present form without access to Soviet sources. During my last trip to the USSR I was able to work in the INION Library in Moscow and at the Akhundov Library in Baku. I consulted with scholars in Moscow, Tbilisi, Erevan, Baku, Tallin, and Tartu, and, in 1984, with scholars in Tashkent and Samarkand as well. Participation in professional conferences in New York, Washington, Madison, London, and Paris was equally beneficial.

Special mention must be made of some of the Soviet publications—including such radically different journals as the scholarly *Sotsiologicheskie issledovaniia*, the popular *Ogonek*, and the

Estonian *Raduga*—which since 1985 have provided a wealth of pertinent information and excellent interpretations.

Finally, my personal thanks go to my daughter Monique for her initial editing, to Eileen Obser and Ann Bramoff for word processing, and to Patricia Kolb, my editor at M. E. Sharpe, Inc.

Soviet Society Today

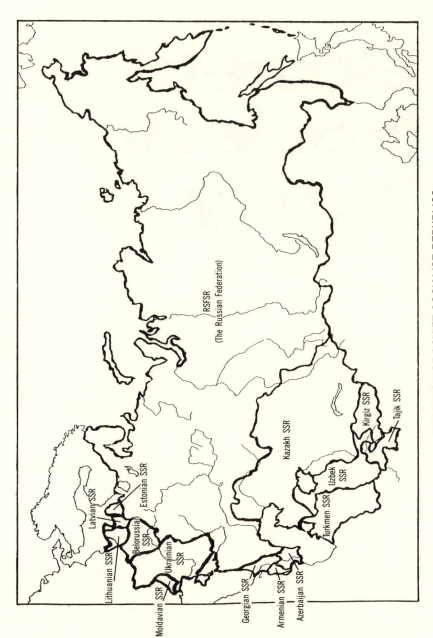

THE UNION OF SOVIET SOCIALIST REPUBLICS

1

Introduction

Is the Soviet Union an equitable, egalitarian society that has reached an unprecedentedly high stage of human development and created a new, better, socially motivated human being? Or is it a totalitarian society, governed by the Communist party elite with a cynical disregard for the common man whose interests it claims to represent?

Is it a bureaucratic regime entangled in red tape, entrapped in endless shortages, and engulfed in a sea of lies and deceptions? Or is it the dynamic creation of a revolutionary social experiment, sometimes faultily executed, but nevertheless scientifically conceived, and capable of correcting its own mistakes?

Is it a modern industrial society, not unlike all the others in its socioeconomic development? Or is it modern in only a few selective fields, while functioning largely at the level of a third world country?

All these questions come to mind when one attempts to analyze Soviet society, but none of them is easy to answer. The social order created after more than seven decades of the Soviet regime is complex; it is full of contradictions and enormous variations, and both positive and negative elements.

Westerners facing the problem often succumb to following preconceived notions or viewing Soviet society as a single entity, disregarding the social, regional, ethnic, and other differences that inevitably characterize a country as large as the Soviet Union. To describe the Soviet way of life without underlining the deep-rooted differences in living standards and lifestyles reduces the scope of inquiry to Moscow and its surroundings, areas better known to tourists, foreign journalists, and scholars.

Today it is impossible for any informed person to accept the old, official Soviet view of the USSR as a conflict-free society, made up of two nonantagonistic classes—workers and peasants— plus the *intelligentsia*, a stratum of educated people who do not fit into either of the two "legitimate" classes. But by the same token, to see the Communist party elite as the only beneficiaries of the regime, disregarding both the rise of the Soviet middle class and the progress of lower classes, is equally unrealistic.

In analyzing Soviet society, one must recognize the tremendous social progress accomplished during the years of the Soviet regime. The population as a whole has been educated (albeit unequally), largely urbanized (not denying all the negative aspects of rapid industrialization), and taught to cherish basic egalitarian principles (even if these are often violated). Over time, and after many painful social upheavals, every citizen has been assured a minimum standard of living encompassing such basic elements as the right to education, employment, shelter, basic health services (granted all these are far from adequate), and a degree of social mobility.

Today, a substantial middle class has unmistakably emerged between the official "workers' state" on one side and the privileged party elite on the other. Middle-class values are increasingly accepted as the norm by all segments of Soviet society, to the detriment of both official values and values traditionally held dear by other social groups. Ethnic differences within the middle class do lead to variations in lifestyles, but without altering the common nature of aspirations shared by the middle classes of all the national groups.

On the other hand, it must be said that the Soviet way of life, based on a "scientific" ideology, bureaucratism, and militarism, has an institutional flavor; standardization prevails throughout the land, affecting everything from offices to grocery stores. There is a dreary monotony to restaurant menus, store window displays, and furniture, to give just a few examples. But despite the stamp of sameness created by institutional conformity, regional differences are deep, ranging from the Middle Eastern atmosphere in the Muslim republics of the south to the Central European feeling in the Baltic republics in the northwest, from the eerie nostalgia of decaying Leningrad to the nondescript modern bedroom cities encircling most metropolitan centers.

Thus, a visitor to the Soviet Union is faced with two apparently contradictory impressions—one of oppressive institutional sameness and one of lively local and ethnic differences. Sometimes one or the other prevails, but often the visitor seems to be viewing two very different but superimposed slides.

What makes the study of Soviet society even more complicated is that it has been formed not through the natural evolution of traditional social structures, but through social experimentation imposed on a basically conservative society—or, more accurately, societies. Of the social groups that existed before the revolution only two—the bureaucracy and the intelligentsia—have survived, despite the repeated purges of their members. For better or worse, their new cohorts have embraced the ways of their Imperial Russian predecessors and are, to some extent, their true heirs.

The peasantry, the predominant prerevolutionary class, which accounted for over 80 percent of tsarist Russia's population, was shaken to its roots when agriculture was collectivized in the late 1920s. Families were forced to join kolkhozes (collective farms) and work practically as farmhands, retaining possession of only the family house and the garden plot around it. The peasantry lost the rest of its land, its elite was deported and resettled, its work ethic was shattered. The mass movement of peasants out of the villages and into the cities, which followed collectivization, left behind the less adaptable, the elderly, the less motivated. Old peasant traditions failed to survive; new ones failed to take hold. As a result of modernization, industrialization, and collectivization, the peasant class, at least in the Slavic republics, lost its position as the repository of national values and no longer fulfills its traditional role as the class base for the social pyramid.

The working class was affected in a different way. At the outset of the Soviet regime its role was glamourized. The relatively tiny revolutionary proletariat was supposed to dominate other social classes and was given relatively high pay and continuous official recognition. But power slipped from workers' hands early on. The working class's dominant position was usurped by the bureaucracy governing in its name, its high pay neutralized by the privileges of that same bureaucracy, its status by the better connections of the growing middle class, and its social standing belied by the nonrecognition of its preeminence by other classes.

The Soviet middle class inherited little from the past. It is not the heir of the old prerevolutionary bourgeoisie but an outgrowth of middle-level bureaucrats and intellectuals. It includes professionals, "achievers" from the tertiary sector (services, trade, etc.), and some elite workers and peasants. Its distinguishing features are the aspirations of financial security, material well-being, and social respectability. Basic material needs are a given, and an acceptable standard of living is taken for granted.

At the top of the social pyramid is the *nomenklatura*—the Communist party elite—in the position occupied before the revolution by the old nobility. Neither hereditary nor wealthy, as the nobility was, it nevertheless enjoys privileges, manages to bestow its status on its children, and retains the monopoly of top civil service (something the old Russian nobility had been progressively losing during the last decades of the empire).

The Soviet class system preserves a sense of social justice and a degree of social mobility. Privileges and high earnings are resented and rarely flaunted, and climbing the social ladder is still possible. The ideal (if not the reality) of social equality still prevails.

According to the revolutionary ideology, equality was also supposed to prevail among the many nationalities of the country. But with time the Russians reemerged as "first among equals," and among the non-Russians some groups gained ground while others lost in status.

Among the more than one hundred nationalities of the USSR, some are large nations, such as the Russians (half the country's population) and Ukrainians (over 50 million people), while others, like the small Siberian native groups, number only in the thousands. Russians, together with their fellow Slavs, the Ukrainians and Belorussians, constitute three-quarters of the population, and non-Slavs the remainder. Among the latter, the largest group is made up of 50 million Soviet Muslims (about 17 percent of the total population of the country), including six large nations with their own union republics: Uzbeks, Kazakhs, Azerbaijanis, Turkmens, Tajiks, and Kirgiz. The other important groups are the Christian nations of the Transcaucasus (Georgians and Armenians), the Baltic nations (Lithuanians, Latvians, and Estonians), the Romanians of Soviet Moldavia, the remaining Finnish groups of northern Russia, the native peoples of Siberia, and, finally, Jews, Germans, and Gypsies. These last national groups are relative newcomers, having appeared within the confines of the Russian empire during the reign of Catherine the Great. The Jews found themselves in Russia by hazard of history, having settled in the parts of Poland annexed during her reign.

Traditionally, the Russian elite took a strongly differentiated view of the various nationalities of the empire, respecting some of them, having little regard for others, trusting some and mistrusting others, co-opting some while keeping others at a distance. Germans (concentrated in the Baltic and Volga regions) were always well regarded. Ukrainians were liked, but their language and culture were belittled. Georgians were essentially trusted; Armenians were tolerated, but less respected than the Georgians. Nomadic Muslims, Siberian natives, and Gypsies were looked upon as primitive. Settled Muslims were better regarded but still seen as semi-barbaric. Poles were mistrusted, and Jews were both disliked and persecuted.

It is ironic that after an initial period of total equality following the revolution, old national prejudices seemed to reappear, sometimes in virulent form. Antisemitic tendencies in Russia,

Armenian-Azerbaijani conflict in the Caucasus, assertions of national pride among the small Baltic peoples, and disregard for Ukrainian and Belorussian culture have all been front-page stories in our own time.

Soviet society is a complex structure made up of social classes peculiar to its system and a wide array of nationalities following their own cultural paths. What makes it all even more difficult to analyze is the fact that the country has now entered another period of profound social change. The process of reevaluation and "restructuring" of the system inaugurated by Mikhail Gorbachev has unleashed long-suppressed social forces and social tensions. The reforms themselves have sometimes followed zigzag paths, with some proceeding much farther than ever anticipated, some being reversed, and others failing to take effect at all.

Almost certainly, a description of the Soviet Union of today will be outdated within a few years. Yet any effort to project an image of the Soviet Union of tomorrow would be premature, and probably incorrect. Socioeconomic reforms tend to produce unexpected results, often contrary to original intentions. Thus a report on contemporary Soviet society can only contrast the present with the past—and with the promise of the future.

The Background

2

Russian Tradition

Russians are the dominant nationality within the Soviet Union, and their traditional moral formation plays a large role in the ways Soviet society functions. Like the traditions of other nationalities, Russian traditions were not eradicated by the revolution. Some were temporarily put aside, others deformed, but their impact remains, and a proper understanding of the present Soviet way of thinking cannot be achieved without due knowledge of its old Russian roots. The tsarist past shaped the future of the new society no less than Marxism did; indeed, in many ways Marxism was made to bend to Russian tradition:

• a strong respect for rank (*chinopochitanie*), unequaled in Europe outside of old Prussia;

• a tendency to look to an "important person" (*vazhnoe litso*) to intercede in a variety of matters;

• a world view based on the struggle between good and evil rather than compromise (a St. George vs. the dragon syndrome);

• a propensity to associate freedom with anarchy;

• a need to believe in a righteous cause;

• an acceptance of suffering as a normal life occurrence.

Respect for rank predates the time of Tsar Peter the Great. Russian aristocrats (boyars) fought for their "rightful" place at the head of the tsar's table, and special lists of boyar families were published, ranking each in order of importance. Court protocol, appointments to administrative positions, marriages—everything was subordinated to the ranking of noble families and their social importance. Peter went even further by establishing a "Table of Ranks," which equated civilian ranks to military ranks. Special formulas were prescribed for addressing ranking officers or bureaucrats. The governmental bureaucracy was dressed in uniforms, as were students and schoolchildren.

A short story by Anton Chekhov, "The Fat and the Thin," about a chance meeting of two old schoolmates, gives an excellent account of the situation still prevailing at the turn of the twentieth century. The lower-ranking friend is so awed by his old chum's unexpected status that he cannot conduct a normal conversation with him.

What is special in the Russian respect for rank is the custom of servitude toward superiors and a compensating rudeness toward subordinates. Talking back to higher-ups is not a Russian habit. Passing the scolding down has been the traditional approach.

The revolution initially dealt a blow to ranks, medals, honors, titles, and the whole set of social relationships based on such distinctions. But old customs die hard. New ranks, medals, titles, and honors soon appeared, and with them came the restoration of a social order based on rank distinctions. Certainly, a general is no longer "his excellency," but "comrade general" is treated not much differently from his tsarist ancestor.

A party first secretary in a provincial town fares not worse than the city governor in Gogol's play *The Inspector General*. A Soviet factory director carries no less sway among his staff than his Western counterpart does, since employees are very conscious of ranking within the enterprise. But the mixture of traditional awe for rank with revolutionary egalitarian principles produces curious results. While many ordinary citizens resent the privileges granted to the *nomenklatura*, few question its status.

Directly connected with the respect for rank is the role of the "important person" in Russian society, a role that has successfully survived all the regime's shifts and changes since the revolu-

Voices

"Once I heard a psychologist define our society as a 'paternalistic society,' with the father crowning the social pyramid. From this comes our civil infantilism, . . . the inability to use our own rights, the naive belief that the 'Supreme Father' will settle the matter in any conflict."

From a discussion in *Literaturnaia gazeta*, June 6, 1988

tion. It is based on people's belief that an important person, regardless of his field of competence, can successfully intercede in any matter, however remote from his area of expertise. In tsarist times, a respected high official would hold reception hours at his town house, where crowds of petitioners swarmed around him with a variety of requests. Thus, a general might be asked to arrange for a job in an old people's home, a postmaster to help with a litigation, or a judge to intercede for a school admission.

Similarly, in the Soviet Union, a party secretary might be approached for any possible reason—an academic admission, an apartment allocation, priority for buying a car (bypassing the usual waiting lists), or getting somebody a job selling soft drinks in a streetcorner booth (a lucrative position in a Soviet city). Generals, directors of large enterprises, and other "important persons" can also intercede, often by using their access to the party committee, or sometimes directly impressing whoever has the power of decision in a given matter. This practice is alien to the West, where a high-ranking person in one field generally holds little sway in another. Still, Soviet emigrants in the United States sometimes try to take this approach to a problem, appealing for support to people who, despite their relative importance in some other field, have nothing to do with the one at hand.

The role of the "important person" is even greater in the non-Russian southern belt of the USSR, from Central Asia to the

Caucasus. The powerful "father figure" is seen as a kind of universal protector capable of distributing favors of all kinds. In the United States the closest comparable figure might be a Mafia godfather or a Tammany Hall boss in old New York. But such a comparison may not be very valid, since the Russian (or Muslim, or Caucasian) "father figure" is rather a respectable person, rarely involved in shady dealings of any kind.

Another traditional Russian characteristic is the view of life as a struggle between good and evil. The very name of Russian Orthodoxy conveys an intolerance of competing views. The Russian church was traditionally intolerant toward other faiths and toward dissenters from its own mainstream. Old Russian epic poems celebrate struggles between righteous heroes and evil villains, with the latter mostly pictured as being of alien races and religions. Compromise between the two is impossible; it would be like a compromise between God and Satan. Struggle can only result in evil's ultimate defeat.

This particular trait of the traditional Russian mentality has persisted. During the revolution, when many old values were—at least temporarily—discarded, this one was only reinforced. True, the definition of what is positive and what is not was altered (the status of royalty and the church switching from good to bad), but the principle of struggle between good and evil was an essential part of the new political life. Everything polarized: revolution vs. counterrevolution, Reds vs. Whites, socialism vs. capitalism, secret police vs. spies and saboteurs, and so forth. Always, the forces of righteousness were set against those of evil, and no compromise was possible.

Struggle was a constant theme during Stalin's time. There was no neutral ground: anyone who displeased the Leader was automatically an enemy to be stamped out. To agree with 99 percent of the official line instead of 100 percent became unacceptable. Writers were compelled to depict the world in black-and-white terms, as in an American cowboy movie in which heroes and villains are clearly identified the moment they appear on the screen. Every character had to be either positive or negative,

Voices

"The primordial natural passions . . . have atrophied here. . . . It is universal that what is alive moves, develops, perfects itself; but here everybody strives for something unchanging, stagnant, static. And whenever some foreign body appears, in the form of a talented, or simply lively, agitated individual, immediately there is an antithetical force to expel the outsider."

From a discussion in *Literaturnaia gazeta*, June 6, 1988

with few if any shades in between. Complex, Dostoevsky-type characters were no longer favored.

Another traditional Russian belief is the equation of freedom with anarchy. In many popular stories, freedom leads directly to license—license to get drunk or go on a rampage. Unchanneled human forces tend to go astray, with disastrous results.

Some interpretations of Russian history provide a great deal of support for this point of view: periods of weakened central authority inevitably ended in successful foreign invasions. Disunity among Kievan princes facilitated the Mongol conquest, the Time of Troubles invited Polish occupation of Moscow. On the other hand, strong autocratic rulers such as Ivan the Terrible, Peter the Great, Catherine the Great, and Stalin have been revered for building Russia's strength.

Even in our day many people, though aware of Stalin's despotism, still laud the discipline prevailing in his time—the way some Germans, not especially fond of Hitler, still praise the "order" he established on the ruins of the "rotten" Weimar Republic. Thus, the fear of anarchy among the Russians is a genuine one, reinforced by the weakness of democratic traditions in the country. To be sure, democratic institutions did surface at times. Russian history offers the examples of the old Novgorodian *veche* (town meeting), the Moscow boyar *duma* (a kind of Russian House of Lords), the nineteenth-century *zemstvo* (local assembly), and finally, the centuries-old peasant *mir* (communal self-government). But by Western standards, Russia's democratic institutions were mostly short-lived and weak. The lesson of Russian history was that free Novgorod lost out to autocratic Moscow. All this led to a lack of proper framework for the development of free institutions, posing a real challenge for democratic reformers in the Soviet Union today.

Another age-old Russian characteristic is the seemingly compulsive need to keep faith in something, though the Russians have changed the object of their devotion over time, each succeeding cause erasing the previous one and, in turn, mandating total allegiance. Those fighting for the revolution had the strength of faith of seventeenth-century Orthodox Old Believers. Faith in Stalin was no weaker than the old faith in the Tsar. Even today, in discussions about the differences between the American and Soviet ways of life, Soviet citizens often reproach Americans for lacking a carefully specified ideology and a well-defined common purpose that could be the focal point of everyone's aspirations. To say that exactly this freedom from conformity is the basis of our way of life does not persuade many Russians.

The problem with an uncompromising cause is that it tends to justify any means that might be necessary for its achievement. All the bloodshed during the revolution and the civil war was sanctified by the Cause, something Boris Pasternak in his novel *Doctor Zhivago* refused to accept, being unwilling to blame only the "wrong" side. The cruelty and sufferings of Stalin's time were seen as the price for building a future paradise, and the generation that bore this burden was dismissed as the "fertilizer of history." Such Western conceptions as freedom of choice, absence of a state religion (or ideology), and the primacy of individual fulfillment over general social goals remain fundamentally alien to Russian tradition.

Another Russian characteristic that has played both a positive and a negative role in shaping Russia's destiny is the much-

Voices

"Social inertia is the reverse side of bureaucratism. . . . The conservatism of the bureaucracy has joined forces with the mood of those at the lower levels, i.e., you and me. There is sentimental reminiscing about the past, a longing for the boss and for order, an instinctive preference for what is usual and traditional. . . . This is the fear of independence. . . . This is the fear of life. . . . Here is where the principal danger to restructuring lies."

From Vasilii Seliunin, "Sources,"
Novyi mir, 1988, No. 5

vaunted capacity to withstand hardship. This attitude enabled Russian soldiers to fight under the most wretched conditions, peasants to cope with oppression, and forced-labor camp inmates to endure terrible privations. But the other side of the same coin is less favorable. Russian pride in the ability to endure suffering has led to passivity in the face of oppression, a passivity strengthened by a belief in the inevitability of suffering in human existence. This brings to mind the famous answer given by Archpriest Avvakum, the seventeenth-century Old Believer who fought the reforms in the official Russian church and suffered persecution. To his wife's question "How long, Archpriest, are we to suffer?" he replied, "Until our very death."

Classic Russian literature is filled with images of human misery, injustice, beatings, oppression. Reading the novels of Dostoevsky, Nekrasov, Saltykov-Shchedrin, Turgenev, and Gorky, to list just a few among the better-known classic Russian writers, one gets a Dickensian dose of human misery.

What is lacking in Russian tradition is the notion of suffering as something abhorrent rather than ordained. True, during the era of serfdom sporadic revolts shook the Russian countryside (most notably the uprisings led by Stenka Razin and Emilian Pugachev), but these flare-ups were followed by centuries of submission.

The October revolution was a most potent revolt against oppression, but the speedy reimposition of autocracy by Stalin was no accident of history. It could be understood as a return to normalcy, with the degree of oppression increased as if to compensate for a temporary relaxation. The inmates of Stalin's camps, the peasants driven into collective farms against their will, the frightened intellectuals awaiting nighttime knocks at the door, all accepted their fate in what must seem to a Westerner a most fatalistic manner.

It is this combination of historically transmitted Russian cultural values—servility toward those in higher positions, suspicion of freedom, rejection of compromise, and fatalistic acceptance of suffering—that makes reform in the Soviet Union today such a difficult task. And this despite democratization, urbanization, modernization, and the technological revolution, which have undeniably altered the very nature of Russian society.

3

Soviet Ideology

The impact of ideology on Soviet life is not easy to describe, since ideology permeates all aspects of life but commands little devotion. Although it occupies a position comparable to that of religion in medieval Europe, it receives mostly lip service from no longer enthusiastic believers.

Militant during the revolution and the civil war, the subject of vigorous debate in the 1920s, with the coming to power of Joseph Stalin, communist ideology increasingly slipped into rhetoric. It was in the name of ideology that Stalin purged the leading lights of the Bolshevik party, his potential rivals and competitors. And it was under its banner that he turned to mass-scale social engineering, uprooting millions of people, transforming their existence to fit his vision, and altering their traditional work habits. Decades later, by the time Brezhnev succeeded Khrushchev, the dust had settled. But revolutionary communist ideology became ever more routinized and disconnected from reality. The incentive to build a new world was gone, and the spirit of innovation had been stamped out. Since the 1930s, and especially since World War II, a measure of Russian nationalism has been periodically added to Soviet ideology in the hope of shoring up its declining vitality.

At the roots of Soviet ideology is Marxist theory, adapted by Lenin to Russian circumstances and known in the Soviet Union under the name ''Marxism-Leninism.'' Karl Marx's thinking was inspired by the French revolution and the Paris Commune, by German philosophy, especially the writings of Hegel, and by the early British economists who bore witness to the industrial revolution in their country, then the most advanced industrial nation of the world.

The two bases of Marxist philosophy are dialectical and historical materialism. Materialism proclaims the primacy of matter over spirit in the universe. Dialectics, with roots in ancient philosophy, is a conceptualization of development. Change is thought of as progressing through the clash between a "thesis" and its "antithesis," resulting in a "synthesis." At this point the synthesis becomes the new thesis, and the whole process starts anew, albeit at a higher level. Thus change proceeds in a spiral-like fashion, with stages repeating themselves, each time at a higher level. Curiously, in Soviet writings the term "dialectical" has often been invoked to justify what seems illogical, just as a religious spokesman might appeal to faith when discussing what seems unexplainable.

Historical materialism applies the principle of materialism and the dialectical method to the understanding of change in human societies. The economy, or "mode of production" in a society, is seen as basic, while nonmaterial components, such as the political system, religion, or simply fashion, are relegated to the "superstructure," able to prevail only as long as their economic foundation remains in place. Over time the emergence of new modes of production must inevitably strain the bonds of the old production relations. Changes in the base eventually bring it into contradiction with its superstructure, which then is bound to be overturned.

In this way, humanity progressed over the millennia from primitive to slave society, then to feudal, and eventually to bourgeois society. Bourgeois society is based on private ownership of the means of production (exploitable land, factories, mines, stores, anything that can produce "value" when labor is added), considered by Marx as the basis of exploitation of man by man and class by class. The capitalist reaps the "surplus value," i.e., profits, which then can be reinvested to acquire new means of production and thus further increase the capitalist's profits. In this system workers are little more than tools that have to be paid only enough to allow them to subsist and reproduce.

The next stage is the socialist one, built on the common ownership of means of production. The replacement of capitalism by socialism through a workers' revolution is seen as historically inevitable, akin to childhood giving way to adulthood. It can be postponed, but not avoided.

Each period in the development of human society has its own ruling class. According to Marx, in the prehistoric classless society of "primitive communism" land ownership was unknown and means of production practically absent. In the slave societies of ancient Greece and Rome, slaveowners ruled, and compulsion dominated production relations. Under feudalism, lords of the manor ruled, while serfs supplied labor in return for a lord's "protection." Finally, under capitalism, the means of production belong to the rich and workers are kept in "wage slavery."

At the socialist stage of development, exploiters are eliminated, labor rules, and the means of production belong to the society as a whole. Still, idleness is not tolerated ("he who does not work, neither shall he eat," proclaims Marx). Each person is supposed to work according to his ability and be compensated accordingly, not equally.

Finally, at the last and highest stage, that of communism, social classes will disappear, and each individual will "work according to his ability and receive according to his needs." Thus the future communist society is a kind of successor to primitive communist society, albeit at an infinitely higher level. Both are classless, with no private property; the first because of its primitivism, the second because it has achieved an overabundance of goods and a high degree of social consciousness. Accumulation of goods is no longer necessary, nor is money, since it serves no purpose; everything is free, and work is voluntary. Governments, with their bureaucratic apparatus, their police, prisons, armies, and other agencies of force, are no longer needed and wither away. There is no want, no struggle, no social conflict under communism. It is the last and highest stage, the perfection of social development. It is a paradise on earth.

For nineteenth-century Russian socialists, the difficulty with Marxist theories was that Russia was not an advanced capitalist industrial nation and therefore—if Marx's scenario was correct—not a candidate for socialist revolution, much less communism. England might qualify, or Germany, but tsarist Russia, with its predominantly illiterate peasant population, was only halfway along the path from feudalism to capitalism. If Russia was a candidate for revolution, by rights it should have been a bourgeois revolution on the French eighteenth-century model.

It was Lenin who overcame this obstacle and legitimized Russia's candidacy for socialist revolution without waiting for it to complete the capitalist stage of development. To achieve this, Lenin styled his Bolshevik party as the "vanguard" of the revolutionary proletariat, destined to lead Russia's small working class and backward peasantry. In October 1917 Lenin's party seized power from the weak bourgeois forces that had come to the fore when the tsar abdicated his throne in February of that year, in the midst of World War I. Since the industrial working class was not large or highly developed, it was not the people but the party-controlled state that ultimately took control of the means of production. And, within a few years, the regime would reclaim most of the vast Russian empire, diluting still further the strength of the Russian working class in the vast ocean of the empire's many peoples.

Thus, perhaps, it should come as no surprise that Marxism-Leninism's most lasting appeal has been not to the workers in the advanced capitalist countries but rather to those in backward, often war-ravaged countries who are fed up with the old, corrupt ruling elites.

Since the victory of the Bolshevik revolution, the "science of Marxism," as developed by Marx's friend Engels and "perfected" by Lenin, has maintained a quasi-monopoly on the official Soviet intellectual scene. For years, Stalin's name was associated with those of the founding fathers, but his greatest contribution was to turn Marxist-Leninist philosophy into a rigid dogma, no longer to be discussed and developed but only learned

Voices

"Since the early 1930s and practically until just recently, we were in a state of intellectual self-isolation. Already the third generation of Soviet historians remains largely ignorant of the trends in the humanities and social sciences abroad. We have lived without Durkheim, Weber, Toynbee, Freud, Croce, Spengler, Braudel, Sorokin, Marcuse, without Collingwood, Jaspers, Altshuler, Jakobson, . . . Carr, Saussure, Trubetzkoy, Boas—I could continue this list for a long time. They are, in their own way, summits of non-Marxist thought, with all their shadows, from light to dark, and they belong to world culture. To know them is a must for every educated humanist."

From a discussion in *Istoriia SSSR*, 1988, No. 1

and recited. The building of Marx's future communist paradise was the goal that justified whatever policies Stalin ordained, no matter what human sufferings they caused, just as it would be invoked by Stalin's successors to legitimate stagnation. All non-Marxist philosophy was rejected as unscientific, branded anti-Soviet, and deemed dangerous for Soviet readers. The result was the isolation of Soviet intellectual and cultural life from what was taking place in the rest of the world and rejection of all "bourgeois" theories, from Freud's psychoanalysis to Einstein's relativity.

It is only under Gorbachev that Soviet scholars have been allowed access to the ideas that have shaped our modern outlook. Still, Gorbachev must move cautiously, for if the official ideology crumbles, what will be left to legitimate his party's rule, and what future goals will justify the sacrifices he must call upon the people of the Soviet Union to make today?

The System

4

The State as Owner

It is difficult for a Westerner to comprehend the extent of state ownership in the Soviet Union. The Soviet Constitution lists the following as state property: land, mineral wealth, water, and forests, the principal means of production in industry, construction, and agriculture, the means of transportation and communication, the property of trade, communal, and other enterprises set up by the state, and the principal housing stock.

Private ownership is basically restricted to household objects, items of personal usage, comfort, and housekeeping, family dwellings, and savings from earned income.

All the land belongs to the state. Thus, even collective farms do not own their land but enjoy a right of perpetual usage. Privately owned single-family houses and dachas (country cottages) are built on state land assigned for usage to the owner of the house. The latter has a title to the house but not to the land on which the house stands, although the land obviously goes with the house in case of sale. Under the personal usage principle, ownership of more than one house or dacha cannot be allowed. Whatever else is connected with a property, whether mineral rights or water resources, cannot possibly be privately owned.

The second kind of state property is that of ''means of production.'' This includes all kinds of plants and factories, mines, commercial fishing and offshore rights—in sum, the totality of industrial activity, except for some very minor, recently allowed initiatives, such as the processing of industrial waste by small cooperatives.

Transportation and communication systems are owned by the state. This includes all railroads, airlines (there is just one, Aeroflot), bus companies, postal services, telephone and telegraph lines, longshore operations, trucking, and taxi fleets; everything except some recently allowed individually owned taxis.

All banking, all wholesale trade, and almost all retail trade (except market stalls) is also in the hands of the state. This means that, minor exceptions aside, every shop door leads to a state-owned establishment.

All important repair shops and service outlets are state-owned. Although lesser ones may officially be cooperatives, most old-style cooperative enterprises have been integrated since 1959 into the state system and managed along public ownership lines, so that they are distinguished from state enterprises in name only.

Hotels, apartment houses, theaters, movie houses, stadiums, and all kinds of urban buildings, except for some single-family dwellings and tool sheds, are also owned by the state. In the countryside the situation is different: private dwellings prevail, and many nonprivate ones are owned by collective farms rather than by the state.

Restaurants, cafeterias, and cafes are predominantly state-owned and state-managed. But many enterprises have their own eating facilities, a few cooperative restaurants have recently appeared, and some private or cooperative food vendors are seen on street corners.

What remains outside the domain of state ownership, not counting the fictitious old-style cooperatives, are the following:
• new-style cooperatives, established since Gorbachev's ascent to power. These include a very limited number of small restaurants, car repair shops, apartment repair crews, and special services ranging from babysitting to horseback-riding lessons;
• individual nonagricultural labor, limited to a single family. Before Gorbachev's reforms this was confined to private lessons, housepainting, tailoring, cleaning, and similar activities. But

now it also includes individually owned taxis and a much larger variety of small technical repair jobs;

• private plots of collective farm members and "garden plots" of urban dwellers. Private plots are legally part of kolkhoz (collective farm) land, state property assigned to the farm in perpetuity. Products grown on private plots, which are usually about half an acre in size, as well as domestic animals raised there, can be freely sold by the peasant. Garden plots in the countryside are officially assigned to urban dwellers to encourage growing garden vegetables on previously uncultivated lands. In reality, they often serve as a pretext for the construction of summer cottages (or even of genuine secondary residences) for more prosperous urbanites. Garden plots are not assigned on a first-come, first-served basis, but through the workplace and special connections, as short-supply goods generally are;

• kolkhoz market stalls, used by peasants to sell products they received for kolkhoz work or produced on their private plots. Other stalls sell foodstuffs produced by the collective farm itself and are not part of "private initiative";

• flower stands in many urban centers where privately grown flowers are offered to passersby;

• selling one's own car (or spare parts) at a second-hand car "flea market";

• selling personal belongings (clothing, furniture, household objects), privately or at a flea market;

• subletting a room in one's apartment;

• tailoring or sewing on individual orders, with the customer supplying the fabric.

In addition, other activities are being "tolerated" but can often border on illegality:

• transporting passengers in private cars, a common phenomenon (in Moscow a taxi ride costs a flat fee of three rubles during daytime hours, and more at night);

• selling neighbors' products (instead of just one's own) at the kolkhoz market. Legal if it involves doing a favor for your neighbor, illegal if it involves reselling at a profit;

• renting a room in a dacha, or in an apartment located in a resort area, where there is generally a shortage of vacation lodging. While occasional renting out may be legal, permanent boarding-house-style renting is not. However, authorities tend to overlook the situation;

• using factory equipment and metal waste at the place of work to produce small items (keyholders, souvenirs) after normal working hours;

• car repairs done after working hours by auto mechanics employed by state repair shops (who often supply otherwise unobtainable spare parts as well).

As far as an individual Soviet citizen is concerned, state ownership of means of production goes far beyond ownership itself. Being the owner of the quasi-totality of workplaces, the state is also the exclusive employer, since no individual, including those now legally engaged in private work, is permitted to hire outsiders (immediate family members are the only exception). In China an individual entrepreneur can hire two workers or five apprentices. In Poland all limits on hired labor have been lifted. But this is not the case in the Soviet Union, at least not yet. The only possible way to hire an outsider is for domestic service—as is still done by the upper strata of Soviet society.

Thus, anyone looking for urban employment has basically one prospective employer in mind—the state. True, the latter presents a multitude of faces—from government offices to community kindergartens, from steel mills to factory cafeterias, from department stores to newspaper stands. But ultimately the employer is one and the same.

Given the diversity of employment possibilities, a conflict at the place of previous employment may not have any serious impact on an employee's ability to find another job. But if the conflict has the slightest political implication, an applicant's whole career may suffer, since the personnel departments of prospective workplaces will be informed of the negative report from the original workplace. Such was the lot, for example, of many of those who were denied permission to emigrate from the Soviet Union during the later Brezhnev years. Fired from their jobs, these ''refuseniks'' had little prospect of getting rehired in a similar capacity.

5

The Bureaucracy

Bureaucracy is no less a characteristic of the Soviet system than state ownership of the means of production; indeed the first follows from the second. Lenin feared that bureaucratization might flourish under the new system, but he could never have predicted its extent.

Russia's prerevolutionary history is rich in bureaucratic tradition. Tsarist bureaucracy dates from pre-Petrine times, taking its roots in the *prikaz* system of administration, in which the boyars (nobles) were assisted by *diaks* (officials) acting in the name of the crown in matters under their jurisdiction. Those dealing with the *prikaz* found to their dismay that the ways of justice are crooked and the waiting time is long. Such Russian expressions as "put into a long drawer" testify to the old tendency to bury every file under a pile of documents, from which it could be extracted only after the proper bribes had been distributed into the right hands.

Peter the Great abolished the old system and created instead a German-style professional bureaucracy charged with precise responsibilities within a much better defined sphere of competence. The bureaucratic apparatus itself was divided into fourteen ranks, each legally equivalent to a corresponding military rank. Bureaucrats, like officers, were to be addressed in accordance with their ranks as "your nobility," "your high nobility," "your excellence," and "your high excellence" and were dressed in appropriate uniforms, showing the color of the particular administration.

The new system was clearly superior to the old, but soon managed to acquire the same torpor and corruption. It survived, with some modifications, until the revolution, when it was abolished and replaced by the new Soviet system. Old titles, ranks, and uniforms were eliminated, and the new system was supposed to reflect the egalitarian principles of socialism.

The reality was different, however. With the state takeover of the private sector, the reach of the new bureaucracy went far beyond that of the old one. And with the punishments inflicted upon a reluctant citizenry grown harsher, bureaucracy's power over people's lives grew accordingly. Party members who clung to revolutionary traditions were soon eliminated by Stalin as hindrances to the new order. The bureaucratic system spread over the totality of the country's life, from the party's secretariat to the management of the corner bakery.

The amount of paperwork originated by Soviet bureaucracy surpasses not only what was typical in prerevolutionary times but what would be imaginable in any contemporary capitalist country as well. There are documents, certificates, permits, passes, directives, acts, regulations, and rules for every conceivable endeavor. The system is busy requiring, affixing, posting, churning out papers of every kind and entangling the population in a web of red tape. No individual initiative goes unsmothered.

The key problem of Soviet bureaucracy lies in the burden it creates for the national economy. The movement of goods and services is severely handicapped by endless paperwork, contributing to the constant shortages that plague Soviet life. The decision-making process is equally bungled, with immobility replacing action; bureaucrats are reluctant to take responsibility for any kind of decision without securing the approval of all the channels involved. Moreover, paper results become more important than real ones. A factory director is first of all preoccupied with the reports he can send to his superiors and to local party bosses, and

Voices

"In management theory there is the concept of a 'self-sufficient system.' When an organization takes excessive management functions into its hands, the number of administrators sooner or later reaches a certain critical magnitude and the apparatus begins to work for itself: the higher-ups write, and those at the bottom make formal replies. Real life is ignored because it only gets in the way. . . . Every year [the bureaucracy] prepares a hundred million sheets of documents, i.e., approximately one page per capita per day. At least 90 percent of the papers are useless—are simply not read by anyone.

. . . more than anything else, bureaucrats are concerned with self-preservation or, what is the same thing, the preservation of administrative methods of management. . . . The existing bureaucratic machine . . . can be broken (which happens with revolutions from below), it can be abolished (as in revolutions from above), but it cannot be restructured."

From Vasilii Seliunin, "Sources,"
Novyi mir, 1988, No. 5

less so with the real state of affairs at the factory. It is said that in the Soviet Union central planning substitutes for market forces, but it might be truer to say that paper accounting takes the place of production and distribution.

Bureaucracy is everywhere, affecting small repair shops and mammoth heavy industries. Passports, passes, and certificates of domicile, of good conduct, of employment, are constantly needed. Mere money cannot buy building material for a dacha, or a voucher for a resort hotel, or a new car at list price. The bureaucratic machine first has to furnish necessary papers allowing the purchase of the desired item. And these papers will not be secured unless the party organization, the workplace, and a number of other institutions agree to back the request. This can generally be secured through connections, influence, or bribes, sometimes by a combination of factors.

Large factories use "pushers" who cajole, threaten, wine, dine, and bribe those in whose hands rests the power to allocate needed resources, machinery, raw materials, or spare parts. It is often the only way to cross the bureaucratic thicket, a jungle rendered impenetrable by confounding regulations.

The Soviet bureaucracy stretches across several social groups. Gorbachev spoke of 18 million people employed in the command-control system, a number nearly on a par with the total party membership, and forty times higher than the total of top *apparatchiki*, the famous *nomenklatura*. Socially, bureaucrats range from high officials down to minor clerks. Of course, one cannot compare the importance of a top manager with that of a ticket clerk in a railway station. But due to the constant shortages plaguing the Soviet economy, each can assert considerable power over hapless citizens. And both can extract some profit from their privileged positions, adding a substantial "fringe benefit" to their official compensation.

When we speak of bureaucratic resistance to *perestroika*, it is not only because the bureaucrats are afraid for their comfortable jobs. There is an embedded resistance to anything new and unfamiliar. In Russia, historically, such resistance has been overcome through drastic action only. Men like Peter the Great and Joseph Stalin wrought change at great human cost. Whether such action can be avoided in today's more civilized circumstances remains to be seen.

6

The Party

The fact that the USSR is a one-party state and that the party in power rules according to Marxist-Leninist principles is so well known that it barely needs additional comment. What is much less understood is that, except at the very top, the political role of the Communist party is minimal. The party's entire mission is centered on administrative and socioeconomic matters, with its purely political activities reduced to enforcing, explaining, and propagandizing policies adopted at the top.

The party has developed into a very large institution numbering over 18 million people (15 percent of the labor force; over 6 percent of the total population of the country, or nearer to 10 percent if those under twenty-one are excluded). At the bottom, it is made up of primary cells and primary organizations. The next step is a party committee, whose jurisdiction covers a specific administrative territory (district, city, or region). In a large city, the city party committee is ranked above the district party committee of its component districts. A city party committee of a small town, on the other hand, will be ranked below that of the district, since the district might include more than one small township within its borders. A regional party committee is ranked above all these and supervises party committees of the cities and districts of the region. At the top is the central committee of the given republic, headed by a presidium and a secretariat.

Finally, at the very summit of the party system, in Moscow, there is a presidium of the All-Union Central Committee (called the Politburo) and a Secretariat. These are the genuine centers of

Communist Party Membership

1917	c. 250,000
1924	472,000
1939	2,307,000
1952	6,708,000
1966	12,357,000
1986	18,300,000

political power in the country, and their members, like those of lower committees, are coopted rather than elected. It is too soon to say how Gorbachev's introduction of multiple candidate elections will affect party governance.

Each party committee, at every level from district to all-Union in Moscow, has a corresponding governmental body—an executive committee—forming the following parallel pattern:

Party	**Government**
City Party Committee	City Executive Committee
District Party Committee	District Executive Committee
Regional Party Committee	Regional Executive Committee
Presidium of Republic Central Committee	Republic Council of Ministers
All-Union Central Committee, Politburo, and Secretariat	All-Union Council of Ministers

Executive committee members at all levels are officially selected by elected popular assemblies or "soviets." These revolutionary institutions were powerful in 1917 and 1918, but soon they lost all their clout and became rubber stamps. Today, all important officials in the executive branch are party members and subject to party discipline.

The parallel structure of party and governmental organizations is a key feature of the system, one that fosters the proliferation of bureaucratic machinery and creates administrative bottlenecks.

Voices

"This year in Arkhangel'sk an election was held for the position of deputy to the Supreme Soviet of the RSFSR. . . . Listed on the ballot as candidate for deputy from our electoral constituency to the republic's highest governing body was Comrade P.

I fulfilled my civic duty and took part in the election, but in the process I began to have certain doubts. Personally, I have nothing against the candidate as a man. It is possible that he is in fact a wonderful worker and a worthy Communist and altogether deserving of great confidence. But as a voter I do not know him. There were no meetings during the preelection campaign between the candidate and a broad audience of his constituents. And in the biography of the candidate which the election organizers presented to the voters for their consideration, much was vague and incomprehensible. Where does the candidate work and what is his occupation? I quote from his biography: '. . . an official in a department of a state agency,' 'works purposefully and unflaggingly in the sector in which he is head.' Doesn't it seem to you that information on the candidate's activities is somewhat lacking?

What's more, it remains a mystery as to which labor collective in our electoral precinct showed such high confidence in Comrade P. to nominate him its candidate for deputy, and when. The biography informs us: '. . . elected a member of the regional committee of the CPSU and a deputy to the regional soviet of people's deputies.' I don't know how he has performed while a deputy to the regional soviet. . . .

The people's representation in the parliamentary bodies of the republic and the union, and likewise in the local soviets, must be truly the people's."

From a letter to *Literaturnaia gazeta*, June 10, 1987

The problem is that, originally, the party was supposed to be a political organization devoted to ideological matters and to keeping the country on a politically correct course, while the governmental side was supposed to administer the country. Lenin himself took the post of the head of the government; the position of the party's general secretary was created only in 1922. The role originally assigned to the general secretary was to register the decisions taken by the Politburo and to see that they were being carried out, not to head the party and the government.

It was by using all the opportunities provided by this key bureaucratic position within the party that Stalin rode to power. In doing so, he reversed the original roles, making the general secretary the head of the Politburo instead of its arm and reducing the Council of People's Commissars (later renamed the Council of Ministers) and its chairman to simple executors who were powerless to settle even minor matters. This state of affairs lasted until the beginning of World War II, when Stalin himself took on the chairmanship of the Council of Ministers, while remaining general secretary of the party. After the war he gave up the latter post to his aide Malenkov, retaining only the governmental position. This was an obvious effort to restore the importance of the Council of Ministers, something only a man of Stalin's stature could afford to do without fearing loss of control over the party machinery.

Stalin's successors could not afford to copy this move and relinquish the key position of general secretary. So the chairmanship of the Council of Ministers again sank to secondary importance. (The current chairman is Prime Minister Nikolai I. Ryzhkov, who is, of course, a member of the party's Politburo.)

Party secretaries have always been the bosses of ''their'' respective domains, permanently condemning their government counterparts to subordinate positions. The same relationship prevails throughout the entire structure down to district levels. The head of, say, a cattle-breeding department of a district party committee clearly ranks above the head of the same department in the district executive committee. The very fact that the party

Leaders of the Soviet Union (years in office)

Vladimir Lenin	(1917–1924)
Joseph Stalin	(1924–1953)
Nikita Khrushchev	(1953–1964)
Leonid Brezhnev	(1964–1982)
Yuri Andropov	(1982–1984)
Konstantin Chernenko	(1984–1985)
Mikhail Gorbachev	(1985–)

committees include so many economic departments is evidence of the role played by the party apparatus in directing the everyday economic affairs of the locality. The power of the corresponding governmental departments and the autonomy of industrial, commercial, and agricultural managers is thereby reduced.

Gorbachev has sought to remove the party from economic matters, to enhance the role of governmental institutions, and to "democratize" and revitalize political life. Potentially the most significant change is the creation of the new Congress of People's Deputies. The delegates chosen in competitive elections in the spring of 1989 include a significant percentage of non-party members and party "mavericks" like Boris Yeltsin. Henceforth it is the Congress that will choose the Supreme Soviet (with its two chambers, the Soviet of the Union and the Soviet of Nationalities, a Presidium, and a President).

Within the party itself, apart from party functionaries whose power is obvious, there are several layers of party members. At the bottom are rank-and-file members, those with modest jobs and limited connections. Then come the party elites, professionals, middle managers, and intellectuals. At the top are those in important command-control positions, people whose names are registered on special lists kept in district, city, regional, and republic party committees (the higher the committee of registry, the more prestigious the list, and the more important the status of

Voices

"Not far from where we live [in Tiumen] they built the so-called 'Obkom' dachas [for regional party committee members]. This considerable stretch of green space, here within city limits, is guarded by the police; a whole staff of service personnel has been assigned, excellent roadways were laid. . . . We assume that all this is legal . . . but maybe it is out of sync with an era of democratization."

From a letter to *Komsomol'skaia pravda*, August 3, 1988

the person on that list). Important managerial vacancies are filled from such lists, and executives already on the job cannot be fired without due hearing at the party committee, from whose list they were selected in the first place.

Those on the lists are known as the *nomenklatura*, the very elite of the system, the "noble class" of the regime. An important factory director or economic trust manager will, as a rule, be a party member of *nomenklatura* standing. Those who are not are excluded from top positions. Whether Gorbachev's experiment in letting some enterprises elect their own directors will change this situation, allowing non-party members to advance to positions of executive responsibility on the basis of their leadership skills and technical competence, it is too early to judge.

In the Soviet Union today, belonging to the party and even holding a high-ranking position in the party may have little to do with ideology. A French or an Italian Communist party member is presumably ideologically committed, or at least opposed to perceived social injustices of the capitalist system. His Soviet counterpart may share this kind of commitment but most often is ideologically indifferent. Communist ideology, familiarity with the "classics" of Marxism-Leninism, belief in the dogma, are of secondary concern. What attracts someone to the party may be sheer opportunism, or just an honest desire to put one's abilities to use, neither of which is normally possible without a party membership card.

In the liberal professions, from medicine to art, one can advance without a party card, although party membership will speed such advancement. But in government, the national economy, agriculture, the armed forces, academic administration, and numerous other fields, absence of party status means limited opportunity. As a result, one can find a good number of able and honest people who joined the party not only to advance their careers but to be able to put their considerable talents to practice.

Our U.S. immigration authorities, who for a long time have created complications in admitting Communist party members to this country, are apparently unaware that a party card may have little significance beyond identifying its holder as someone adept at climbing the social ladder.

7

The KGB

The Soviet institution that holds perhaps the most fascination for Westerners is the infamous KGB—the Committee for State Security, a Soviet combination of our FBI and CIA under one roof.

The origin of that organization goes back to the beginnings of the revolution. On December 20, 1917, only a few weeks after the Bolshevik victory (and less than ten months after the liquidation of the tsarist secret police, the "Okhrana"), an Extraordinary Commission for the Suppression of Counterrevolution, known by its Russian initials as the "Cheka," was created. Its first chairman was a Polish Bolshevik, Felix Dzerzhinsky, son of a wealthy landowner, and a faithful follower of Lenin.

On February 22, 1918, during the very dangerous moment of German advance prior to the conclusion of the Soviet–German armistice at Brest-Litovsk, the Cheka issued an order to seek and shoot on the spot enemy agents and spies, counterrevolutionary agitators, organizers of revolts, speculators, suppliers of weapons to the White forces, and turncoats attempting to join the White opponents of the revolution.

The Cheka enjoyed an almost free rein with the lives of the citizenry until December 1921, when some curbs were finally imposed on its activity. Until then, mass executions of all kinds of real or perceived "enemies" of the regime, pickpockets, "reactionary intellectuals," or just unlucky bystanders were frequent occurrences. The difference between life and death was often in the hands of a Cheka agent operating with a bare minimum of restrictions. Some well-known Russian writers were saved from the firing squad by a timely intervention of their pro-regime colleagues; others were less fortunate.

On February 8, 1922, the Cheka was replaced by a new organization, the GPU (State Political Administration), later renamed OGPU (Unified State Political Administration). The newly reformed entity was to be supervised by the procurator general and subordinated to the Council of Ministers. Dzerzhinsky stayed at the helm of the OGPU until his death in 1926. His deputy, Viacheslav Menzhinsky, also a Pole, took over and led the organization until his own death in 1934.

The OGPU directed its activities against all kinds of real and imagined enemies including leftovers of the old bourgeoisie, ''NEP'' men (private entrepreneurs allowed to operate during the short-lived New Economic Policy of 1922–1926), ''bourgeois intellectuals,'' and ''kulaks'' (prosperous peasants). It was during the collectivization drive and the mass arrests of kulaks and deportations of their families that the OGPU became the largest employer in the country. It ''took care'' of millions of inmates in the Siberian camps, which it supervised.

In July 1934 the OGPU was replaced by a new organization with, this time, a ministerial status—the NKVD (People's Commissariat for Internal Affairs). Its competence was far-reaching, extending beyond state security to include such varied domains as civil registry, fire departments, highway administration, frontier guards, internal security troops, convoy troops, and penal institutions.

The new boss, Genrikh Iagoda, was no longer a political figure like Dzerzhinsky, just a police official. He barely lasted two years. In September 1936 he was arrested and replaced by Nikolai Ezhov, who in turn was arrested two years later. Both Iagoda and Ezhov were involved in the most extensive purges, mass arrests, and deportations the Soviet Union had ever seen and were most probably liquidated for knowing too much about the entire unholy operation. Lavrenti Beria, who took over the organization in 1938, after Ezhov's demise, managed to become a powerful political figure but failed to survive Stalin's reign. He was arrested and shot not long after the death of his protector, in 1953.

Structurally, the NKVD under Beria was divided in 1941 into two separate administrations. The old NKVD was deprived of state security functions and remained essentially in charge of regular police activities. The new NKGB (People's Commissariat for State Security), which in 1946 became the Ministry of State Security, or MGB, was entrusted with state security. Temporarily reunited in 1953, the two were split again two years later.

At that time a new reorganization took place. The dreaded "troikas," special three-member MGB boards which judged purported "state criminals" in the absence of the accused or his lawyer, were disbanded. Security troops were shifted to the jurisdiction of the Ministry of Defense. Road and highway administration was entrusted to the Ministry of Road Transportation.

After the fall of Beria, the MGB—abolished as a ministry and renamed the Committee for State Security, or KGB, its present name—was no longer in a position to terrorize party officials and returned to its initial purpose of being an instrument in the hands of the party leadership. But the short-lived ascension to power of Yuri Andropov, for fourteen years head of the KGB, to the position of general secretary (1982–1984) was proof that a KGB connection was still a plus in a political career. Since then, however, the KGB has been headed by technocrats with no apparent aspirations to political leadership.

The extent of the KGB's domain can be best illustrated by Western estimates, which place the numbers of KGB personnel at almost 2 million, including KGB troops and the army of part-time informers. The prison population, which until the 1950s was under its supervision, is estimated at 5 million in 1934, 10 million in 1937–38, and between 7 million and 13 million after World War II. In 1953 the camps were transferred to the jurisdiction of the Ministry of Justice, and the name "camp," having too many negative connotations, was changed to "colony."

The enormous Soviet "gulag" system, though surpassed in its

atrocity by the Nazi camps, has been a much more durable institution. While the Nazi camps existed for "only" ten years, Soviet camps have survived for over six decades, with three of the six as genuine "Stalin camps," such as described by Alexander Solzhenitsyn in his *Gulag Archipelago*. The starvation diet, the forced labor (enforced by the threat of even harsher incarceration and further reduced food rations), primitive living conditions, and inadequate clothing resulted in heavy mortalities. Since then, camp conditions have improved, but "reduced diets" are still in use, and living conditions are still unacceptable by Western penal standards.

It is worth noting that the initial intention in establishing "re-education labor camps" was based on the idea of rehabilitating delinquents through training in labor habits. Unfortunately, the original purpose was soon forgotten (except in the case of some colonies for adolescent criminals), and the camps took on very different dimensions. Inmates were mercilessly exploited during most of Stalin's grandiose construction projects, such as the famous White Sea–Baltic canal. Soviet camps supplied armies of slave laborers, reminiscent of those who built the pyramids for the pharoahs, an analogy used by the poet Evgenii Evtushenko in his "Bratskaia GES."

The inscription "*Arbeit macht frei*" (work liberates) would be almost as inapplicable to a Soviet camp as it was to Auschwitz. Though Stalin-era camps were not extermination camps as such, half of the inmates failed to survive the regular ten-year term (twenty-year terms were also common, while five years was considered a "child's term"). Moreover, many inmates had their terms arbitrarily increased, and most of those who were freed were not allowed to return directly home but were placed for a few more years in forced residence in remote areas of the country.

A good picture of the activities of the KGB and its predecessors can be derived from the list of major mass deportations conducted by the state security organs (called simply "organs" in the USSR):

- late 1920s–early '30s: large scale deportation of so-called kulaks from their native villages and resettlement of their families in remote areas of the country;
- mid-1930s: reprisals against "bourgeois intellectuals";
- second half of the 1930s: mass arrests and deportations of "old Bolsheviks," military officers, and ordinary party cadres;
- 1939–40: deportation of former Polish, Romanian, Lithuanian, Latvian, and Estonian citizens from territories annexed by the USSR as a result of the Molotov-Ribbentrop agreement between the USSR and Germany (over a million people were deported from former Polish territories alone);
- 1941–44: removal of several nationalities from their homelands en masse, accused of collaboration and of harboring pro-German sympathies;
- mid-1940s: "provisional" deportation of returning Soviet POWs. Many were accused of collaboration with the Germans; others were kept a few years for "verification";
- 1945–46: deportation of Vlasov army soldiers (former Soviet POWs who joined the German-created Russian army led by Andrei Vlasov, a captured Soviet general);
- late 1940s: deportation of petty offenders accused of minor theft or "speculation," acts severely punishable according to a postwar decree;
- 1950: deportation of prosperous farmers during collectivization in the Baltic region;
- 1952–53: preparations for collective measures against Jews (after the famous "doctors' case"), which were stopped by Stalin's death.

Stalin's death not only interrupted the chain of deportations, but led to a massive discharge of survivors from the camps. Rehabilitation of former victims of Stalinism started during Khrushchev's time and is being completed, thirty years later, under Gorbachev. While "penal colonies" (or camps) still exist, they harbor few political prisoners (probably a few hundred, as opposed to millions in Stalin's time).

KGB methods of control within the country (we are not concerned here about its foreign operations) are:
- a network of "free-lance" informers in all Soviet enterprises, organizations, localities, housing projects, educational institutions, etc.;
- technical or practical surveillance (listening to telephone conversations, reading people's mail, tailing by foot or by car);
- intimidation (calling people in for questioning, veiled or direct threats, calls to employers);
- the presence of special (security) sections within every enterprise of any importance. The section controls employees' records, collects information, keeps in touch with the administration, approves appointments.

What has changed since Stalin's time is not the principle of surveillance, or the extent of the KGB's interests, but the severity of the punishments inflicted and the behavior of KGB agents. Under Stalin, virtually anyone could be arrested for telling an "anti-Soviet" anecdote overheard by the wrong person, terrorized into confession of further "anti-Soviet activity" or even "spying for the enemy," and sent for several years to a concentration camp in remote Siberia, where he would have a fifty-fifty chance for survival.

Today, an anecdote is not enough to bring real trouble, but a protest action may lead to a "conversation" with a KGB official. Hints of losing one's job, being charged with "hooliganism," or undergoing an extended examination in a psychiatric ward may be made during such a "conversation." And those threats would not always be idle.

KGB types have also evolved. Originally, some Cheka agents were revolutionary idealists; others were uneducated brutes using "Red terror" as a way of self-affirmation. With time, both types either died out or were purged. Those who remained adapted themselves and became regular bureaucrats, while numbers of simple opportunists joined their ranks.

The third generation of KGB agents, the one we see now, is educated and professional. Today's average KGB agent sees his job as employment rather than a defense of revolutionary aims or an opportunity for sadistic behavior. KGB work means good fringe benefits (ranging from better housing to special stores) and promotion opportunities. Modern agents are no less efficient than their predecessors in keeping an eye on dissidents, discontented minorities, and outspoken intellectuals. It is simply that methods are more civilized and the punishments more measured.

The enormous building at Dzerzhinsky Square in Moscow, larger than Macy's department store in New York, contains the infamous Lubianka prison and serves as a reminder of the KGB's permanent presence in the capital. The statue of ''Iron Felix'' in the square facing his old headquarters has become a symbol of Stalin's Russia, just as the mounted statue of Peter the Great in St. Petersburg personifies the Romanov empire.

8

The Military

A book on Soviet society has no need for an account of battlefield history or military preparedness, but to omit the Soviet military would leave a gap in the picture of the Soviet social scene. There is probably no other country in the world where uniforms are so much in view, even on military personnel who are on leave, where military service is of such great importance and medals are worn so often, or where past wars have so strong a hold on people's imaginations.

There are several key points to understanding the social importance of the Soviet military:

• It is the Russian national tradition, and not the revolutionary one, that has governed the Soviet army since the early days of World War II;

• The subordination of the armed forces to the party has been, and still remains, the rule of the game;

• The social role of military service in such varied fields as education, national/ethnic relations, and sports is even greater than in the United States.

It was Peter the Great who created the professional Russian army around the year 1700, patterning it on the German and Swedish armies. Strict discipline, respect for rank, and limited personal initiative were instilled in the soldiers from the very beginning. Until 1862 soldiers were mostly serfs, and officers predominantly nobles, a situation discredited by the Russian defeat in the Crimean War of 1854–55. Toward the end of World

War I, the still predominantly peasant Russian army crumbled, with only the officer corps and the Cossacks still willing to fight. This made the revolution possible and, with the victory of the revolution, the birth of the new "Red Army" in February 1918.

At the outset the Red Army, organized by the famous revolutionary leader Leon Trotsky, rejected all the attributes of the old. Ranks, decorations, outward respect for officers, Russian military tradition—everything went overboard. Medals and epaulets were worn only by the counterrevolutionary White forces; the Reds despised them and replaced them with red geometric insignias. Everyone was a "comrade." Saluting was out, and commissars (reliable party men dispatched to the army) were made equal to army commanders—professional military men whom the party did not trust.

The military suffered great losses during the purges of the 1930s. Stalin made a point of keeping the armed forces strong, but under strict control, in order to eliminate all possibility of challenge from that side. In his early struggle for power he eliminated his arch rival, Trotsky, and later, in 1937–39, the majority of the army's high command, including the famous marshals Tukhachevsky and Blucher, as well as scores of others. This decimation of the army command partly accounts for early Soviet reverses following the German attack on June 22, 1941.

The role of the professional army obviously rose in World War II. Commissars lost their equal standing with the commanders, and prerevolutionary ranks, insignias, decorations, and discipline came back in full force.

After the war, Stalin hastily replaced several successful commanders, just to remind the army who was in charge. But after his death, the army high command took an active part in Kremlin power plays, as in the arrest of Stalin's KGB chief Lavrenti Beria (who saw himself as his boss's heir), and in endorsing successive general secretaries. But there has never, as far as we know, been an attempt on the part of the army command either to dispute the party's leadership or to act as a full-fledged interest group. The often expressed Western view about an ongoing rivalry among the party, the army, the KGB, and the bureaucracy for the control of the country's destiny is a distortion of reality, since party members occupy leading positions in all the other bodies as well. It may—and probably does—happen that the bulk of the army's leadership has a preference for a certain party leader as against another, but it is in their capacity as members of the party elite, not as a separate center of power. The USSR is not a Latin American republic ripe for takeover by a military junta.

The romantic view of the Red Army as a popular force, defender of the downtrodden and of the oppressed, and therefore not comparable to ''bourgeois'' armies, remains part of Soviet folklore. Book after book, movie after movie shows revolutionary sailors in their black blouses, munition bands around their chests and grenades at their belts, workers with red armbands, commissars in leather jackets. But today's Soviet army resembles much more the old tsarist one than the Red Army of civil war days; the myth survives as a legend, not as a reality.

One of the critical problems facing the Soviet military today is the growing percentage of non-Russians (particularly non-Slavs) among army draftees, who usually serve between two and three years. The non-Slavic recruits present several shortcomings from the army point of view: lack of feeling for the Russian military glory and tradition on which army morale is based, often poor command of the Russian language, and potential for ethnic confrontations. By the year 2000, over a third of Soviet draftees could be Soviet Muslims, not counting other non-Slavic groups.

On the positive side, the Soviet army serves the cause of integration, improves the knowledge of Russian, and teaches cooperation to young men of different nationalities and cultural backgrounds—something they might otherwise have missed in civilian life. In this respect it is not unlike the U.S. military.

From the perspective of Soviet society, the Soviet armed forces are not just a military machine that marched into Budapest, Prague, or Kabul, but a special social experience affecting the bulk of young men ages eighteen to twenty and playing an important role in their personal formation. Being in the army is a harder experience in the Soviet Union than it is in the United States: the discipline is harsher, the food is worse, creature comforts are fewer, the pay only token, and political indoctrination intensive. Young men of different nationalities are not uniformly affected by army life. It is said that Muslim, Baltic, and Jewish draftees, being sensitive to Russian chauvinism, are usually more immune to the army's integrationist spirit, whereas Slavic ones are generally more positively affected. Whatever the case, the social value of army experience cannot possibly be ignored.

9

The Multinational Dimension

The Soviet Union is a multinational state built by and around a predominant nationality, namely, the Russians. Russian imperial expansion began in the middle of the sixteenth century and has lasted for four centuries. By comparison, the federal principle is much more recent: it started with the 1917 revolution and is barely seventy years old.

The conquest of Kazan and Astrakhan by Tsar Ivan the Terrible, rolling back the remnants of the Mongol Golden Horde, marks the beginning of the massive expansion of the Russian state. The drive was tri-directional. The eastward drive brought Russia to the shores of the Pacific Ocean and to the mountains of Pamir (the former in the seventeenth, the latter in the nineteenth century), making the empire the neighbor of Japan, China, and India. The southern drive led into the Caucasus and ended in the northern dependencies of Turkey and Iran and on the shores of the Black Sea.

The western drive was the most difficult, bearing fruit only at the time of Peter the Great, a century and a half after the beginning of Russian expansion. In the north it ended with the reduction of Sweden to the rank of a secondary power and the conquest of former Swedish dependencies in the Gulf of Finland. The central part of the western drive finally succeeded under Catherine the Great and led to the partition of Poland, for centuries Russia's principal rival in Eastern Europe. The southern part of the western drive brought the Russians to the edge of the Balkans, pushing back the Ottoman Turks. The empire experienced very few irreversible losses like the sale of Alaska to the United States.

Within the borders of the empire only Finland and two Central Asian protectorates, Khiva and Bukhara, maintained any degree of autonomy. The other conquered states or territories were gradually transformed into provinces ruled by Russian governors and civil servants.

Among its promises, the Bolshevik revolution was supposed to end Russian domination of the old empire and even give each nationality the right to self-determination, including the right of secession. But before long these proclaimed "rights" were accompanied by insurmountable restrictions. Thus, "bourgeois" self-determination was out; the interest of the revolution was to remain paramount, and advocacy of secession was seen as akin to treason. As a result, only those nationalities that had accumulated military strength (or outside support) managed to keep their independence once it was initially achieved. Others had their short-lived statehood terminated by the Red Army. The exceptions were the western borderlands, where Finland, Estonia, Latvia, and Lithuania managed to secede from the former empire, while a reborn Poland extended its borders into parts of Belorussian and Ukrainian territory it had lost in the eighteenth century. Small losses to Romania and Turkey completed the picture.

Stalin used the first opportunity to recover lost lands, and few of them survived the 1939 Molotov–Ribbentrop nonaggression pact, when Stalin and Hitler agreed to slice up Eastern Europe between them. The partition of Poland brought back a good part of territories ceded to the Polish state in 1920, as well as Galicia, which was never a part of the Romanovs' empire. Romania was forced to return Bessarabia, and to cede northern Bukovina as well. Lithuania, Latvia, and Estonia were brought back into the fold. Only Finland miraculously escaped that fate, through stubborn resistance and a great deal of sheer luck. Among those affected by the pact, only Poland was resurrected after the war, albeit within the Soviet sphere of influence. The last territorial

---

Union Republics and Autonomous Republics of the USSR

Republic	Capital
Russian Soviet Federated Soviet Republic	Moscow
*including:**	
Bashkir ASSR	
Buriat ASSR	
Dagestan ASSR	
Kabarda-Balkar ASSR	
Kalmyk ASSR	
Karelian ASSR	
Komi ASSR	
Mari ASSR	
Mordva ASSR	
North Ossetia ASSR	
Tatar ASSR	
Tuva ASSR	
Udmurt ASSR	
Chechen-Ingush ASSR	
Yakut ASSR	
Ukraine	Kiev
Belorussia	Minsk
Uzbekistan	Tashkent
including:	
Kara-Kalpak ASSR	
Kazakhstan	Alma-Ata
Kirgizia	Frunze
Tajikistan	Dushanbe
Turkmenistan	Ashkhabad
Azerbaijan	Baku
including:	
Nakhichevan ASSR	
Georgia	Tbilisi
including:	
Ajar ASSR	
Abkhaz ASSR	
Armenia	Erevan
Lithuania	Vilnius
Latvia	Riga
Estonia	Tallin
Moldavia	Kishinev

*The former Volga German ASSR (dissolved in 1941) was located in the RSFSR. The territory of the former Crimean Tatar ASSR (dissolved in 1944) has been transferred to the Ukrainian SSR.

additions made by the Soviet heirs to the old Russian empire were the Kurile Islands off the Japanese coast, Tanu-Tuva (north of Mongolia), and Transcarpathian Ukraine, which was extracted from Czechoslovakia.

The Soviet Union as it is today encompasses almost as much non-Russian population as its predecessor, the Russian empire. But the differences between the two entities are substantial. Today's Soviet Union is divided into fifteen *union republics* (SSRs), each named after its main nationality. Within these republics there are smaller units also roughly corresponding to the boundaries of national groups. Thus, today there are twenty *autonomous republics* (ASSRs), eight *autonomous regions*, and several *autonomous districts*. These are the four levels of national-territorial autonomy existing within the country.

Both union and autonomous republics can, to some extent, be compared to the states of the United States; they have a great deal of say in their own internal affairs. The union republics even have a constitutional right to withdraw from the union, something American states do not have; but this right is absolutely fictitious and not taken seriously by anyone in Moscow or in the republics, although it can be invoked in support of local demands for increased autonomy. Otherwise, a union republic has less political autonomy than a state in the United States due to its total dependency on Moscow in financial matters: a republic collects no income, sales, or real estate taxes, just some limited user taxes. Its budget is financed by centrally distributed allocations, which only partially reflect the revenues collected from its territory.

The governmental structure is duplicated at both federal and republic levels. Within the governmental setup there are three kinds of ministries: federal (all-union), in charge of central matters; mixed (operating at both republic and federal levels); and republican, in charge of minor, local matters only. The party remains one, with each republic's party organization subordinated to the Politburo and Secretariat in Moscow. Thus, the system provides room for diversity but leaves the final say to the Russian-dominated federal level.

As the first commissar of nationality affairs, Stalin was the main architect of the Soviet federal system, while as general secretary of the party's Central Committee he exercised control over staffing policies, which played an equally important role in the evolution of the system. A central component of Stalin's "nationalities policy" was his "national cadres" policy, in line with which specific positions within each republic were reserved for Russians and other trusted groups (Ukrainians, Belorussians, Georgians, and Armenians), while "native" cadres were placed in the most visible jobs. The pattern was to assign a Russian second-in-command to every important native boss. While the "second" (and this includes the position of second secretary in party committees at all levels) was supposed to assist the "first," he was also well placed to sound the alarm in case nationalist tendencies surfaced in the boss's actions.

The presence of non-Russians in the central apparatus of both the party and the government—which had been widespread under Lenin—diminished during Stalin's time and has decreased even further in our day.

Still, not everything in prewar nationalities policy can be considered negative. The egalitarian principle of nondiscrimination, whether against entire nationalities or against individuals, was, for years, successfully enforced.

But certainly a low point in the history of Soviet nationality relations was the deportation to Siberia, Central Asia, and Kazakhstan of entire national groups (Volga Germans, Crimean Tatars, Kalmyks, Chechens, Ingushes, Karachai, Balkars, and Mesketians) suspected of harboring pro-German sentiments during World War II. In the decades since Stalin's death this policy has been reversed, although the Crimean Tatars still have not been allowed to reclaim their homeland. (The Crimean Tatar ASSR was dissolved in 1944, when its native population was deported, just as the Volga German ASSR had been dissolved in

1941.) Today, the condemnation of Stalin's treatment of "punished nations" has led to demands for a more "Leninist" solution of the Crimean Tatar problem.

During the post-Stalin years, and especially during the long reign of Leonid Brezhnev, a kind of *modus vivendi* was reached between Moscow and the non-Russian leaderships in the republics. Under that tacit understanding, Russian domination and the continuation of established ethnic staffing patterns were counterbalanced by permitting local leaders a great deal of elbow room within their own republics. Nepotism, corruption, patronage, and abuse of power were tolerated as long as overt nationalism was absent and obedience to Moscow unquestioned. A good deal of "affirmative action" (to use the American expression) increased the popularity of local party leaders as well.

Gorbachev's commitment to radical economic reforms has put the Brezhnev system under question. With economic efficiency receiving top priority, the old balancing act between central prerogatives and local interests has been dangerously strained. Nepotism and corruption, cornerstones of local life in Central Asia and the Caucasus, were no longer to be tolerated. Massive purges in the Kazakh party organization and the appointment of a Russian to the position of first secretary upset the ethnic balance in staffing in that republic and led to riots in Alma-Ata in December 1986. Local ethnic conflicts reignited in the Nagorno-Karabakh Autonomous Region, a largely Armenian enclave in the union republic of Azerbaijan.

In the western parts of the country, especially in the relatively prosperous Baltic republics, there have been demonstrations demanding economic and cultural autonomy and restrictions on immigration from outside the region. These actions have had considerable support, and even leadership, from the republic party organizations. After all, the same *perestroika* that has unsettled the situation in the Asian republics could justify letting Vilnius, Riga, and Tallin handle their own problems. If economic efficiency is paramount, it can hardly be applied only when it favors Russian cadres.

There are three important factors that one must keep in mind when reviewing the Soviet nationalities picture.

First is the personal equality of opportunities enjoyed by persons of every nationality within the USSR (Jews and "punished peoples" excepted). Thus, although one risks jail for disseminating "nationalist propaganda," there is still relatively little discrimination along the road to personal advancement. Although Russians do occupy strategic positions within the party and government apparatus of the republics, numerically such reserved positions account for less than one percent of available jobs. In most cases, being a native of a given republic helps, rather than hinders, one's chances for advancement, although only within the confines of that republic.

Second, the Russians themselves do not profit economically from holding on to the empire left to them by the tsars. In male/female longevity, average wages, per capita housing space, and many other measures of well-being, the Russian republic lags behind Estonia, Lithuania, Georgia, and Armenia. Lack of economic motivation in playing "big brother" to the Soviet multinational family is contrary to usual conceptions about colonialist behavior.

Finally, in dealing with Soviet nationality problems, one must remember that difficulties exist not only between the Russians on the one hand and the non-Russians on the other but among various non-Russian groups as well. Armenians, Jews, Tajiks, and a great many other groups have some difficulties with their neighbors, as the situation in the Caucasus today well attests. Ukrainians, the largest non-Russian group in the country (unless all the Muslims are counted together), while sometimes at odds with the Russians, still prefer them to any non-Slavs in the country.

Thus the nationalities situation in the USSR is complex, a mixed bag of impressive achievements (such as modernization of formerly backward national groups) and abject failures (such as the deportation of ''punished peoples'' by Stalin). The equality of personal opportunities plus Soviet-style affirmative action benefits non-Russians, whereas the dominant position of Moscow and the presence of Russian appointees in the republics tilt the scale in favor of Russia. A totally negative or totally positive view of the situation is out of the question. Soviet socialism cannot solve the nationality question, which is by its very nature insoluble. Given the complexity of the situation, the best it can hope to achieve is a minimum of failures.

The Social
Structure

10

The New Middle Class

The Soviet middle class is at once the most important and the most overlooked social class in Soviet society. This error originates both in the Soviet self-understanding and in the skewed Western view of Soviet society.

In the USSR the prevailing two-class conception of society (workers, peasants, plus an educated stratum, the intelligentsia) leaves no room for anyone else. Moreover, in Soviet eyes the idea of a "middle class" evokes the term "bourgeoisie," which has a negative connotation as a survival of the past and a class peculiar to capitalism, not a present-day class formation of Soviet society.

In the West, it was an overwhelming interest in the status of the party elite that led analysts to ignore the rise of the Soviet middle class. The *nomenklatura*, which is supposed to number somewhere between 400,000 and 500,000 elite party members in top party, administrative, and managerial positions, has been rightly perceived as the chief beneficiary of the regime. But this elite was seen in direct opposition to the undifferentiated masses of the people.

The intelligentsia is a special category not truly equivalent to what the West would call intellectuals. In the Russian context, this social stratum includes those who in the nineteenth century would have been characterized as *raznochintsy*, educated people of various social origins. Anyone who does not do manual labor and who participates in the cultural life of the society can be classified as a member of the intelligentsia. Such a wide definition encompasses a large number of people, from office clerks to well-known writers, from elementary school teachers to army officers.

In the West, by contrast, the circle of intellectuals is seen as much more restrictive and is limited to what the Russians call the "creative intelligentsia," i.e., scholars, writers, and artists. We even exclude well-paid and well-educated professionals such as doctors, dentists, lawyers, and engineers if the latter are not specifically involved in the creative processes. Thus, in the West, a lawyer who writes on legal subjects may be seen as intellectual, but one who practices his profession in a more conventional sense is viewed as just another specialist. In the Soviet Union, however, every doctor, lawyer, or engineer is seen as a member of the intelligentsia simply by virtue of his education and social standing.

The Soviet middle class encompasses the bulk of the intelligentsia, except for those at the very top and the very bottom either socially or financially. It includes the more skilled and prosperous workers and peasants as well. In that respect it is no different from our middle class, except for two elements. First, given the character of Soviet society, very few "entrepreneurs" are included. A degree of private initiative has been legalized only lately, and those who acquired wealth through entrepreneurial activity were essentially black marketeers, not a respectable social group. Second, it is important to note that Soviet middle-class standards correspond to our lower-middle and middle-middle ones. Those whose standard of living matches that of our upper-middle class can be found only among the top echelons of the *nomenklatura*.

These two restrictions notwithstanding, the Soviet middle class bears a great deal of resemblance to ours. Like ours, it is consumption-oriented, respectful of property, and opposed to administrative restrictions. Indeed, these attitudes are even more pronounced since in the Soviet Union consumer goods are hard to get, property is difficult to acquire, and restrictions abound. A Soviet "bourgeois" likes to shop, accumulate possessions, and

Voices

"Sonia goes to a music school; she practices at a friend's house. Must she get her own piano? She must! I'm the one who bought the piano for my granddaughter. My son's family still lives with us, you see. Is a separate apartment for them a must? It's a must! We are saving up to buy a co-op apartment. . . . and a car? and a dacha? Not long ago Leonid said dreamily, 'When we finish paying for the apartment, let's buy a Zhiguli [car].' And we will."

From *Raduga*, 1987, No. 11

be free to dispose of his money. A nice apartment, a dacha, travel, clothing, entertainment, education for the children, proper social behavior—all these are the normal Soviet middle-class preoccupations, and they are no different from ours.

While general middle-class values may be universal in nature, some regional and cultural differences have to be taken into account. Family well-being and hospitality are of primary importance in the Muslim republics; cars, clothing, and travel among Georgians; a dacha and a car for the Russians, and so on. Still, all the ingredients are present across the board, despite some differences in the order of importance.

As a sociopolitical factor, the Soviet middle class is undoubtedly growing in importance. And inevitably, it gains at the expense of other groups. While the Soviet middle class is far from being as predominant as ours, it is already large enough to have edged into a comfortable position within Soviet society. It is even gaining on the *nomenklatura*, the real ruling class in today's USSR. There is no doubt that of all Soviet social classes, it is the middle class that provides the bulk of support for Gorbachev's reforms.

Without endorsing our own division of society into upper, middle, and lower classes, with each of these subdivided into three subgroups, some Soviet scholars manage to discuss the middle class without calling it that. When we read about people identified as "professionals," "specialists," and "managers," it is the middle class that is meant. The bulk of the 18 million persons categorized as holding "management and control" positions in Soviet society enjoy what we would call a middle-class lifestyle.

The Soviet middle class exists in everything but name. It is growing in size, and its importance increases proportionately. Sooner or later Soviet social scientists will feel free to acknowledge what they know very well already.

11

The Working Class

To be a worker in the Soviet Union is to be a sort of master-servant; it is a unique status that requires some explaining to a Westerner. In everyday life it is not much different from being a worker in a capitalist country with similar per capita incomes (say, Portugal or Greece). In theory, the worker—although no longer the official master of the country, as he was supposed to be during the initial period of the "dictatorship of the proletariat"—is still considered to be "number one" on the political ladder. But on the social ladder he occupies a low rung. Moreover, the Soviet worker lacks some basic rights enjoyed by his capitalist counter-part, among them the right to strike (workers are not supposed to strike against a "workers' state").

Working conditions in the Soviet Union have changed over time. Immediately after the revolution, to satisfy workers' demands, the workload was lightened, working hours were reduced, and workers were given a voice in running the plant. However, with the introduction of five-year plans in 1926–27 and Stalin's crash industrialization effort, workers were made to work harder, their role in running the plant was reduced to a formality, and "shock work" programs were introduced, forcing workers to stay at the job beyond regular hours whenever necessary to fulfill the production plan. Aleksei Stakhanov, a coal-miner who "overfulfilled" his quota, was held up as a model for every Soviet worker. In 1940 the situation got even harder: a governmental decree specified fines and even jail terms for three accumulated absences or latenesses, and changing jobs without authorization was prohibited.

The war years, obviously, increased the demands made upon workers: the draft exemption granted to indispensable workers was seen as a privilege, and Herculean production efforts were expected in return. The immediate postwar years failed to lighten much of the burden: Stalin imposed heavy jail terms for minor theft (including "taking" small items from the plant), something that had been largely tolerated for years to allow the worker to supplement his devalued salary.

After Stalin's death, the situation gradually improved. Not only were the 1940 decrees withdrawn and the devalued currency exchanged at ten to one, but labor shortages in many areas made management more receptive to workers' complaints. In time, many skilled workers managed to improve their working conditions greatly: management needed them badly to fulfill the plan and was ready to show a great deal of tolerance. The work tempo was slowed, latenesses and absences went unpunished, work breaks became longer. After-hours "side jobs" and "taking" from the shop were once again overlooked, except in the most extreme cases. The work week was reduced to forty-two hours.

Thus, during the Brezhnev 1970s, the Soviet worker got used to exerting less. Without either Stalin's stick or the capitalist's carrot, there was more incentive to preserve one's energy for after-hours jobs than to work hard at the plant for much less additional income. However, in the southern belt, an area with a labor surplus, and many industries that rely heavily on female labor, the workers had a much harder time and earned much smaller wages than workers in heavy industrial areas.

Another peculiarity of Soviet working conditions is the existence of the "labor book" (described in a later chapter), the limited role of the labor union, and the fact that wage rates are all set centrally, in Moscow. Despite some regional adjustments, wage rates are basically standard for the same job categories across the land.

Voices

"Until recently in our metal industry the trend was toward continuously increasing the volume of production. Now we produce more steel than the United States, West Germany, Great Britain, and France combined, but despite this we still have a shortage. And this is not surprising: our steel is generally of poorer quality. . . ."

From *Lichnaia tochka zreniia* (Moscow, 1987)

The system of pay of the Soviet worker is also different from ours. While monthly (rather than weekly) wages prevail in some job categories, and hourly wages in others, many workers are paid under a system based on production quotas, with each percentage point over the norm raising the compensation, and each percentage under lowering it. For a long time, this piecework system was lauded in the USSR as economically progressive and conducive to better performance, while our hourly wages were seen as outdated. However, when workers were pushed to over-fulfill the plan in terms of quantity, quality was neglected. Sloppy workmanship, massive percentages of rejects, and squandering of raw materials became the trademark of Soviet industry. At this moment, Gorbachev is shifting industry to hourly wages, with an emphasis on quality and cost efficiency.

Gorbachev's reforms have, for the time being, enjoyed only limited support among workers. Some are discouraged by the prospect of having to work more and with greater diligence for less real pay, and with no immediate expectation of improvements in the supply of consumer goods. Others simply resent the skyrocketing price of vodka, an essential pleasure in the dreary lives of Soviet workers, in short supply in recent years.

The paradoxical nature of a worker's life in the Soviet Union is a special problem. Being a worker by origin is a political plus for

Voices

"We unlearned how to grow wheat, or to use an ax, or to screw simple bolts; instead we hammered them down. . . . We failed to mix something into our paint, to pour something into our glue, to dry our wood, to grease our machines. And, as a result, other capable nations no longer buy what is made by our negligent hands."

From *Literaturnaia gazeta*, April 20, 1988

those who are climbing the career ladder and leaving the old work shoes behind. But to remain a worker is a social dead end. Educated people regard a marriage between a blue-collar worker and anyone but a peasant or another worker as an obvious mismatch, and many Soviet novels revolve around this issue. Workers are perceived by the middle class as crude, lazy, simple, and often drunk, and as such not much different from peasants.

The American social acceptance of manual work as something one can be proud of is not characteristic of Soviet society. In the eyes of the Soviet middle class, educated people are not supposed to dirty their hands, and doing so carries a social stigma. This despite the fact that Soviet workers' salaries have risen faster than those of white-collar employees, even engineers. It thus often happens that the very same person who looks down at the worker makes much less money than he does.

For schoolchildren, the decisive moment for future social class standing comes at graduation from the Soviet equivalent of our junior high school, when the less successful students are pushed toward vocational education and away from academic high schools. Parents are told about the honor befalling their children who are asked to join the prestigious working class. Parents do know better, however, and try their best to reroute their sons and daughters back on the "middle class" track.

12

The Peasantry

There is probably no harsher chapter in Russian social history than the one dealing with the fate of the peasantry. Today's Russian *kolkhoznik*, or collective farm member, is only five generations away from serfdom. His grandfather lived in a world of communal landownership (the *mir*). His father, barely having left the *mir*, underwent the trials of revolution, civil war, and war communism, followed by the respite of the New Economic Policy, during which private farming was allowed, and finally, in the late 1920s, the tragedy of collectivization.

The kolkhoznik learned the hard lesson that neither he nor his aspirations nor his work was to be respected under the new order and that agricultural labor would bring little reward. Not surprisingly, the peasant lost interest in farming, except on the small garden plot still in his family's possession. His own children deserted the village if at all possible and joined the ranks of the urban working class.

The Russian peasantry's decline had its historical roots in the latter half the the nineteenth century. In 1862 serfdom was finally abolished in Russia, the last country to do so in Europe, and the serfs were set free. Prior to this time, Russian peasants were divided into three categories: those belonging to noble landowners, those belonging to the crown, and a minority of free peasants living mostly in Siberia and the Cossack areas, regions where serfdom never took hold. Proprietary peasants were themselves divided into three groups: those working a specific number of days per year on their masters' fields (*barshchina*), those paying their masters in cash or in kind (*obrok*) but otherwise free to dispose of their own time, and those working as servants in their masters' household (*dvorovye*).

Owners of serfs could buy or sell them, but, with few exceptions (the *dvorovye*), only as part of land transactions, and not individually. Peasants lived in their own houses in the villages and were governed by their own communal self-government, made up of peasant elders.

Peasants owned only the land on which their homes stood, as well as the yard and the garden plot around those homes. The rest of the land in and around the village belonged to the community as a whole, and every few years it was redistributed by the *mir* for individual family use. This was done on the basis of the number of males per household; females were not taken into account. The family was free to cultivate, harvest, even rent the land, but could not sell it, since they were not the proprietor—the *mir* was. Forests and pastures around the village were most often in the hands of the landowner, but peasants were customarily allowed some usage for their cattle.

At the time of the abolition of serfdom in 1862, the state created special land banks, which paid the landowners the appraised value of the *mir* land in their former villages. The *mir*, in turn, was given long-term, low-interest mortgage loans which it had to repay. This transaction created a great deal of discontent among the peasantry, since in their perception the *mir* land was never the landowner's property. There was even an appropriate peasant saying: "We are yours, but the land is ours."

The tsarist government, conscious of growing discontent among the peasants, eventually canceled the mortgage payments; but the resentment of having been asked to pay for one's own land persisted. Still, during the years following the abolition of serfdom, the Russian village started along the path toward modernization. In 1910–11 another radical reform took place, one that might have altered the future of the Russian peasantry, and even of Russia itself, had it been given the chance to run its course. Put into action by Petr Stolypin (chairman of the Council of Ministers) and known by his name, this reform gave the peasant the choice to leave the *mir* while retaining the land allocated to his use, and become an owner, free to sell his land at will. (Prior to the reform, the peasant was free to leave the *mir*, but his land remained in the *mir*'s possession.) The Stolypin reform accelerated the transition of Russian agriculture to private farming, and by the time of the February revolution, half of the peasantry had taken advantage of the new law and left the *mir*.

The October revolution was, at its outset, favorable to the peasantry. It allowed the peasants to seize and divide the landowners' estates, thus going far beyond their original aspirations. No attempts were made to salvage the *mir*. But on the other hand, during the years of civil war, the currency depreciated, and there was very little to buy in exchange for foodstuffs. Naturally, this sharply reduced the peasants' incentive to produce for the market. In order to supply the cities with food, the government began to requisition grain from the peasants, paying for it in worthless IOUs. A cat-and-mouse game began, with the peasant hiding his goods and the government agents searching the farms for them.

This situation lasted until the beginning of the New Economic Policy in 1922, at which point a free market in agriculture was permitted. Then a limited private sector was restored in the cities, and the worthless currency was exchanged for a stable new one.

But the good times lasted only five years. The decision to implement a crash industrialization program was accompanied by another to harness the peasantry to this goal, with no possibility of withholding grain from the cities. The five-year plan gave absolute priority to the development of heavy industry, so it was clear that few resources could be allocated to the farmers in exchange for their products. Moreover, the belief was that "socialism" could not be built on the basis of "capitalist" agriculture. By 1927 the collectivization drive was under way.

In carrying out the collectivization drive, the authorities

adopted a divide-and-conquer strategy. They divided the peasant community into three groups: the prosperous peasant (*kulak*), the middle peasant (*seredniak*), and the poor peasant (*bedniak*). The lands and other possessions of the kulaks were confiscated and turned over to the newly created collective farms, or kolkhozes. The poor peasants were the beneficiaries of collectivization, acquiring their rich neighbors' possessions, albeit collectively and not individually. Middle peasants were either persuaded or pressured to join the kolkhozes.

Workers from the cities were assigned as chairmen of the new collectives. In addition, machine-tractor stations (MTS), serving neighboring kolkhozes and staffed by workers, were created at the outset of collectivization with the goal of keeping the "tools of production" in proletarian hands.

But difficulties developed almost immediately. First of all, officials carrying out the drive overplayed their hand by trying to turn some of the newly created collective farms into full-scale communes, with group eating facilities and no private plots. Furthermore, the bulk of middle peasants desperately resisted collectivization, seeing in it a threat to their cherished landownership. Only the poorest peasants, those who had little to lose from any change, had any motivation to join the new experiment.

Faced with all these difficulties, Stalin moved in three directions in 1929. First, it was announced that the family house, garden plot, and a few farm animals would remain in the personal possession of the peasant. Second, the government began mass deportation of kulaks to labor camps and resettled their families in Siberia, Kazakhstan, or Central Asia. Finally, middle peasants, the most numerous group within the peasantry, were progressively forced to join the collective farms. At first, economic pressure was used: ever increasing taxation, "exchange" of their landholdings for less desirable plots, "borrowing" of their farm animals, etc. Then straightforward pressure was applied, culminating in reclassification of some middle peasants as kulaks, and even some unruly poor peasants as *podkulachniki* (kulak's helpers).

Voices

"My childhood was spent in a poor Belorussian village and corresponded in time with collectivization. . . . The difference in our area was that we had no kulaks. . . . Nevertheless we had to carry out de-kulakization. It was impossible to designate anyone as a 'land-grabber' because no one had much land. All the same the village 'de-kulakized' three who were just as poor as anyone else. . . .

I also recall when grain had to be turned over to the collective farm so that the land could be seeded. A commission was created that went from farm to farm digging out every kernel of grain, but even then there wasn't enough to sow, and the suspicion arose that not all the grain was being turned in, that some of the grain was being hidden. And in order that the hidden grain not be made into flour, the local bunglers smashed all the millstones."

From an interview with Vasil' Bykov,
Literaturnaia gazeta, May 14, 1986

By 1933 Soviet agriculture was, for all practical purposes, collectivized, but at a very high cost for the country and an even higher cost for the peasantry. The cattle stock in many areas was decimated: peasants anticipating collectivization had slaughtered their animals, while "collectivized" cattle were often left to starve. It was thirty years before the country as a whole restored its cattle stock to precollectivization levels, and the meat problem in the country has not been satisfactorily solved to this day.

But a much more lasting effect of collectivization was the destruction of traditional work habits in the countryside. The kulaks, depicted at the time as bloodsuckers and exploiters, were in reality mostly hard-working people who, while certainly more prosperous than their neighbors, were not rich by any Western standard. Their demise deprived villages of their most enterpris-

Voices

"We lived in the north, on the Mezen River, where there were dozens of villages, with their fields and pastures and hundreds of horses, cows, and sheep. After the revolution my father received a parcel [of land], cleared the forest and drained the swamp. We had two horses, three cows, sheep. From the spring on, the entire family, and we were nine children, plowed, planted, and weeded the fields, and in the summer we worked from dawn to dusk. But in 1929 my father was included on the list of kulaks, although he never employed hired hands. . . . We were dispersed [deported]. And when many decades later I revisited my native place, my heart bled at the sight of our land, which had turned back into wooded swamp. Out of numerous villages on the Mezen, only a few were left. I saw nothing good in the local kolkhoz either."

From a letter quoted in *Izvestiia*, June 9, 1987

ing element and discouraged the remaining peasants from working hard since success would only bring disaster on a family. Work in the collective farm was viewed as akin to work for the old-time landowner. Only private plots and the few farm animals left in individual ownership warranted better care.

Nor were the collectives left in peace to develop. Kolkhoz chairmen were appointed, not elected, and they were often total outsiders, not only to the village but even to the region and to agriculture as well. The *kolkhozniki* were told what to plant, how to plant it, and at what time, so that all local initiative was quashed. On the eve of the German invasion the government had to dictate minimum numbers of work days to be filled by every collective farm member. Differentiated according to regional conditions (160 days per year, average), the number roughly corresponded to the one used by pre–1862 landowners for serfs toiling on their masters' fields.

The post-Stalin era saw a relaxation of such rules. But at the same time, the villages were subjected to new experiments. First, the machine-tractor stations were liquidated. Early collective farms had had to contract with the MTS for all jobs performed by farm machinery operated by MTS workers. Under Khrushchev, the MTS were finally disbanded and their machinery sold to the collective farms. But the farms themselves were conglomerated to create larger, and supposedly more efficient, units. In fact, this broke the territorial relationship between the village and the collective farm and led to the abandonment of many smaller villages. This only accelerated the depopulation of the countryside, especially in Russia proper.

The next innovation was the Brezhnev-era transformation of many collective farms into state farms (sovkhozes), which turned peasants into agricultural wage-earners. ''Private plots'' were still provided, but in some places peasants were moved into new ''garden-style'' two-story apartment houses, a move that led to the further abandonment of old villages.

Finally, collective farm members were guaranteed a minimum income (a kind of rural minimum wage). This was done to remedy the situation in some farms, where the income distributed was below the amount necessary for any conceivable minimum living standard, thus annihilating any incentive for working in the kolkhoz.

All these measures failed to achieve the desired result. The gap between city and village failed to narrow. While electricity reached most villages, modern sanitation, decent roads, and consumer goods remained scarce. Rural poverty proved hard to alleviate. Young people continued to flee rural life, and more and more villages were deserted. The work crews in the fields were increasingly composed of women and older men.

The demoralization of the Russian peasantry was complete. The work was hard and almost utterly without reward or honor.

Voices

"It all ended with the sorry fact that during the years of stagnation, the productive forces of the village were almost destroyed. Many collective farms were left without members. . . . During the years of bureaucratic harassment and freewheeling, the peasant swallowed all the misery, the promises of bounty, the bosses' curses. [Finally] the toiler spat on all this, and went away wherever the road led."

From *Literaturnaia gazeta*, April 20, 1988

The first priority of the collective farm was to pay taxes to the state, mostly in grain, produce, dairy or meat deliveries; then the wages of salaried people had to be paid; and finally some grain had to be stored for seeds. Theft, neglect, vermin, and spoilage reduced the harvest even further. Often, very little was left to kolkhoz members as compensation for their work days. Moreover, "work days" were not equal to days of work. The production quota which determined the number of "work days" was an unreachable goal for many.

Given the unreliability of kolkhoz income, the peasants had to concentrate their efforts on their private plots. Selling their individually produced surplus in nearby urban "kolkhoz markets" became the principal source of revenue of most collective farmers, as well as a major source of foodstuffs for the population. In 1987, private and garden plots, whose share of the arable land in the USSR is only 2.7 percent, accounted for an astonishing 25 percent of agricultural production.

In general terms, the fate of Russian peasantry was matched by that of their Ukrainian and Belorussian cousins. But in the Baltic republics, Moldavia, the Caucasus, and Central Asia the picture was somewhat different; private initiative showed more strength, and so more of the agrarian work ethic survived. The republics of the southern belt, rich in fruits and vegetables, endowed with a better climate and strengthened by better national cohesion, managed to preserve more elbow room within the collective farms. Today, Georgian and Uzbek farmers travel as far north as Moscow and Siberia to sell their products for handsome profits. The kolkhoz markets in the southern republics are models of opulence for the Russians.

In the Baltic republics and Moldavia, collectivization came late, since these areas were annexed by the USSR in 1940, were under German occupation between 1941 and 1944, and had a few years of respite after the war. Not long after the completion of collectivization in these regions and the deportation of local kulaks, Stalin died and the harshest policies were relaxed. Thus, fortunately, the destruction of the peasants' way of life was neither as intensive nor as extensive. Consequently, the Baltic peasantry, and to a lesser extent the Moldavian, was not as morally damaged as that of the rest of the country. In Estonia, where the work ethic still survives, even the collective farms seem to function properly, providing by far the highest incomes in the country. Private plots appear equally efficient: Estonian private flower-growers even managed to dislodge the Georgians as the principal winter flower suppliers in Leningrad.

Gorbachev, who formerly held the post of Minister of Agriculture, is well aware of the need for a thorough-going agrarian reform. But until recently he stopped short of taking on the failed collective and state farm system, which has long been ideologically sacred. Instead, limited reforms such as the family contract (*semeinyi podriad*) were introduced. This innovation allows an individual family to sign a contract with a collective farm, lease some kolkhoz land on that basis, and work independently, promising delivery of a fixed part of the profit (or harvest). While this is a step forward, it is still not modern, fully profit-oriented private farming. On the contrary, it is reminiscent of the pre–1862 *obrok*, when a peasant was also free to fend for himself on the condition of sharing revenues with the landowner.

The agricultural situation was not improved by such half-measures, and the problem of food supply has grown more serious. In March 1989 Gorbachev proposed a "New Agrarian Policy" (a term recalling Lenin's New Economic Policy of the 1920s). The reform plan calls for the dismantling of the state agricultural bureaucracy, the "radical restructuring" of collective and state farms into family or cooperative leaseholds, the breakup of unprofitable farms, and the gradual introduction of a free market in agricultural products. Gorbachev's proposals in this area, as in others, have excited not only ideological objections but also resistance from those with vested interests in the status quo—namely bureaucrats, farm managers, and those peasants who are content to rely on receiving their minimum income from the farm, seeing it as a sort of sinecure.

Today, the decline of agriculture and the demoralization of rural society are most severe in Russia proper. The proverbial Russian peasant, uneducated but hard-working, simple but trustworthy, the unspoiled representative of the nation's core, was certainly an idealized image. There was drinking and cheating, servility toward the mighty, and cruelty toward the weak. But there was also a great deal of value in the popular image of peasant hard work, piety, and good will.

The new Russian peasant is literate (although often poorly), cynical (not just suspicious as his grandfather rightfully was), and no longer inclined to overexert himself. Some contemporary Russian writers of the "village" school still try to evoke poet Sergei Esenin's "blue and golden" Russia of the past, but the Russian peasantry will never again be the trustees of the national spirit. If any group is, it is the middle class, itself drawn to European cultural and material values.

The Russian peasantry today accounts for just one-third of the Russian population, as opposed to four-fifths at the time of the revolution. But more to the point, the Russian peasantry has lost its resilience and is in need of long-term rehabilitation.

13

The Poor

Poverty is a relative notion, based on comparisons between various levels of the same society at a given time, and not an absolute measure based on some universally established standards. In the United States there are some 29 million people classified as living below the poverty level, or over 12.5 percent of the total population of the country. This figure includes an underclass of about half a million people living at the very lowest level. Yet many, perhaps even the majority of the millions of people considered poor in the United States, might seem quite prosperous from the vantage point of a third world country or, for that matter, the United States of some years ago.

Open discussions about poverty in the USSR have begun to appear in the pages of the Soviet press only since the introduction of Gorbachev's *glasnost* policy. According to Academician Tatiana Zaslavskaia, a leading Soviet sociologist and an ardent proponent of Gorbachev's reforms, the two bottom groups on the Soviet social ladder are the 8.8 percent of the population who fail to manage from paycheck to paycheck (or rather, from pay envelope to pay envelope, since employees in the USSR are not paid by check), and the 24.2 percent of the population comprising the second lowest group, who are barely able to cover basic expenses. Since lodging, however unsatisfactory, is heavily subsidized in the USSR and presents no drain on the budget, "not managing" or "barely managing" to make ends meet means an ability to secure only the most basic food and clothing needs, and no more.

Another Soviet study, based on subjective factors of self-evalu-

Voices

"Some twenty years ago, while working as a correspondent in New York, I wrote more than once about the social dregs there, depicted the truly frightful vices and evils of American society—rich, but merciless to its failures. Even now, whenever I am in New York, I am dumbfounded to see how this giant of a city . . . parades its homeless outcasts, rejects, and unfortunates openly in the streets. One of the paradoxes of the days preceding the policy of *glasnost* is that life in New York was shown to us in greater detail than life in Moscow. But now we see our life better and more thoroughly—and in it, among other things, Moscow's unfortunates. Unfortunate perhaps for other reasons and in a different way; but the socially downtrodden exist even in our society, and only a communal shortage of charity prevented us from noticing them earlier."

Izvestiia reporter Stanislav N. Kondrashov
in *Kommunist*, 1987, No. 14

ation by the respondents themselves, gives even higher poverty figures: 9.8–12.6 percent for the lowest group and 21.2–25.1 percent for the "hand-to-mouth" category.

Slumlike living conditions and a constant lack of money are universal attributes of poverty, but the measures applicable for the Soviet Union are not exact duplications of those that apply in the United States. In an American city a slum dwelling is generally an apartment located in a ghetto or a decaying neighborhood. It is roach- or rat-infested and has walls covered with graffiti. It has broken elevators, mail boxes, and doors, poor security, and filth in the halls. In the Soviet Union, the urban poor live mostly in communal apartments (in large cities, at least one-fifth of the population still lives that way), sharing a kitchen and sanitary facilities with several other families. In some areas the housing lacks basic comforts or sanitation: an outhouse instead of a flush toilet, no modern cooking facilities, often no running water, just a well in the courtyard, and no heating system. The percentage of such dwellings is still relatively large in the Soviet Union. Thus, an American slum building is characterized by squalor and decay but tends to offer basic modern facilities, however neglected. A Soviet slum, on the other hand, is usually the result of objective material factors that good maintenance cannot remedy.

In purely financial terms, the poverty level in the Soviet Union could be characterized by a family income of less than 50 rubles per person per month (or less than 200 rubles for a family of four, with some regional and urban/rural variations). But with money less of a yardstick than in the West, Soviet poverty often results from a lack of access to goods and services rather than from low earnings.

A principal wage-earner who has a meager salary, a job carrying no privileges of any kind, no lucrative connections, and no possibility (or ability) to supplement his income, whether legally or not, will place himself and his family in poverty. Thus, an office worker paid 120 rubles per month, with a wife and two children and no special connections or know-how will remain at the bottom of the social ladder, whereas a grocery store clerk on a similar salary may manage quite well by using his access to short-supply goods to his family's advantage.

The monthly cost of raising a child, age one to seven, is estimated at 90 rubles. Child support given to families with per capita income of less than 50 rubles per month would not exceed 20 percent of the above expenses for the first and 25 percent for the second child, except during the first year, when a 35-ruble monthly allowance is added to the compensation.

The classic example of Soviet urban poverty might be a family with one wage-earner in a job presenting no side opportunities of any kind, living in a communal or otherwise substandard apart-

Voices

"I am twenty, married. We live with my parents. My husband brings home 120 rubles [per month]. I stay home with the child and receive 35 rubles. When I was working we somehow managed. Now we catastrophically lack money. And we would like to have three children. Maybe doctors and professors could show us how we can live on 155 rubles. A baby carriage costs 75 rubles. . . . Diapers, blanket, clothing. And the child grows. Not long ago we bought shoes for me for 38 rubles; we barely made it to the next payday."

From a letter to *Komsomol'skaia pravda*, August 14, 1987

ment, and lacking the personal connections that could enable him to escape his predicament. In addition, alcohol consumption tends to take a disproportionate share of the family income, the drink serving both as a consolation for the householder's troubles and an additional cause for their aggravation. While households headed by a single woman are not typical, they may fare better than ones headed by troubled individuals fitting the above description.

It is important to note that Soviet minorities are not disproportionately represented among the poor. The highest standards of living are in the Baltic republics, Georgia, and Armenia. The lowest are in some areas of Central Asia and in Russia proper, especially in the central region.

As far as nutrition is concerned, the Soviet poor have bad diets, just as the poor in our own country do, but that is where the similarity ends. In the United States, junk food and soft drinks contribute to inadequate nutrition, especially where child neglect is a factor. In the USSR, on the other hand, it is the shortage of proper ingredients in the state stores, combined with high market prices and lack of access to special stores, that deprives the poor of meats, dairy products, vegetables, and fruits. Once more, objective factors seem decisive in the USSR, whereas subjective ones play a greater role in the United States.

Clothing is another chronic problem in the Soviet Union, and an especially crucial one for the poor. Since informal clothing often costs more than formal wear, the Soviet poor most often dress traditionally in well-worn and stained outfits, often bought second hand, or in the cheapest available new clothing. In the United States, where acceptable quality clothing is relatively cheap, informal clothing even cheaper, and second-hand clothing practically free, the poor, on the average, face fewer problems in this domain than do their Soviet counterparts. In both cases clothing betrays poverty, but it is the mediocre quality and poor styling in the United States, the worn-out appearance in the USSR.

In the United States moving out of poverty often means getting off welfare. But welfare as an institution does not exist in the Soviet Union. The government's obligation is to furnish a job, any kind of job, not to furnish aid, except to minors or invalids. An able-bodied person, even with small children, who asks for help will be either sent to a state farm or offered the lowest possible urban job, ranging from street-sweeping to ditch-digging. The children will be assigned to day-care centers. ''Parasites'' who refuse to work can be forced to work and deported to a remote, labor-short area for good measure. These possibilities tend to discourage people from turning to the authorities for assistance.

A jobless Soviet citizen will try to cope either by seeking help from friends and relatives or by trying to make some money privately, on the side, without involving the authorities in any way. The reason is simple: unemployment officially does not exist, and a person claiming to be unemployed

Voices

"My wife and I are sixty-three. She hasn't been well since she was a child. As I said, she was a farmhand. She's been sick all her life. Myself, because of illness, I was unable to reach the required twenty-five years of work. As a result, we were left without a pension. I ask the local agencies: Let me have a pension, even if only 20 rubles per month. As a worker with an incomplete work record.

Dear Comrades! Understand me well: The problem is that we have no children, and it really is very, very difficult for us financially. Believe me, if we had someone to finish our life with, we would not bother the newspaper because of those 20 rubles. Despite my sickness, I was not lazy, and have worked."

From a letter to *Izvestiia*, September 2, 1987

could easily find himself bringing in the harvest in a potato field.

While official unemployment data are not published, figures in the millions are heard of in the southern belt, especially for Uzbekistan, Tajikistan, and Azerbaijan. On the other hand, the Baltic republics, the Moscow and Leningrad regions, and Siberia have no unemployment whatsoever.

Underemployment is a common Soviet phenomenon, a tradition dating from the 1920s, when numerous artificial jobs were created in order to end unemployment. Although some of these jobs disappeared in the course of Soviet history, many still linger. Any Westerner who visits a Soviet hotel, restaurant, or office cannot fail to notice the large number of superfluous employees filing duplicate forms, sitting by elevators to watch who comes and goes, and holding up the restaurant walls. On the city streets one sees people sweeping up dirt with little vegetable brooms, selling subway passes, or offering to weigh visitors, to mention only a few of many urban occupations.

Still, not all the underemployed are poor. Some superfluous jobs carry access and connections compensating for low salaries. But those who are less lucky and have to subsist on marginal wages, somewhere between 80 and 120 rubles per month, join the ranks of the poor, sharing the same shortage of prospects with the rest of the ''lower lower class.''

14

Social Mobility

At the outset of the Soviet regime, social mobility was the rule, not the exception. The slogan "he who was nothing will become everything" said it all: not only were the old ruling social classes dispossessed, but their children were barred from all advancement. The proverbial "son of a charwoman and four handymen" was to be the man of the future.

Former nobles, clergymen, merchants, officers, and state functionaries were classified as *lishentsy* (deprived ones). They were not allowed to vote or to occupy positions of importance unless they redeemed themselves by service to the cause during the revolution and civil war. Their children could not enter universities. The words "son or daughter of a landowner or merchant" were sure to close all doors, whether in employment or education. The 1924 Soviet constitution legalized this discrimination.

Gradually these restrictions were lifted, and the 1936 constitution removed most of the legal limitations imposed on members of the old upper classes by giving them the right to vote (symbolically an important privilege, even though voting was virtually meaningless). But wrong social origin remained a barrier to advancement in most cases.

As a result of this direct discrimination (and the exodus of a good part of the possessing classes to the West during the revolution, the civil war, and the early 1920s), very few representatives of the "old families" managed to accede to leading positions in the new society. Thus, by World War II, the bulk of Soviet managers, functionaries, and intellectuals had been recruited from among workers and peasants, a case of phenomenal social mobility.

Beginning with the postwar years, everything began to change. First of all, social origin gradually lost its importance, to the point that today even an old Russian title (an anathema in the 1920s and an obstacle in the 1930s or 1940s) is a plus rather than a minus as far as employment is concerned. More important is that the new managerial class, although predominantly of worker or peasant descent, promoted its own children no less assiduously than the possessing classes did before the revolution. As a result, it was becoming more and more difficult for workers' sons to move ahead, despite repeated governmental attempts to ease their admission to institutions of higher learning.

In the 1920s "workers' faculties" (*rabfaki*) were set up to allow workers who had not completed a high school education to acquire technical or engineering skills at the college level. Graduates of such schools had technical knowledge, though they generally were poorly educated in other respects. Such establishments no longer exist. The preference shown working-class children in admission to universities today is akin to that given to U.S. veterans and not much more. This is not enough to allow most of them to compete against the better-prepared middle-class applicants. Moreover, good connections can make a difference. Children of managers or party functionaries have the right pull; workers' children may have formal claims but their chances of realizing them are poor. In the Baltic republics, for example, between 38 and 54 percent of the students in institutions of higher learning are children of "specialists," i.e., of middle-class origin.

Promotions at the workplace underwent a similar change. Before World War II, most Soviet managers were promoted from the ranks of the workers. Nowadays they tend to be college-educated and to come from professional families. The earlier types are becoming a rarity.

**Slowdown of Social Mobility
(data from 1980, in %)**

	Professionals with higher education		
	ages to 29	ages 30–44	ages 45 +
Parents were workers or peasants	36	49	65
Parents were white- collar workers	25	20	13
Parents were professionals	39	31	22

Source: A. V. Kirkh, "Intergenerational Social Mobility among the Urban Population," *Sotsial'naia mobil'nost' gorodskogo naseleniia* (Tallin, 1985).

Khrushchev tried to shake up the situation by forcing high school graduates to work for two years prior to entering college. This project was one of the causes of his downfall: party function-aries were averse to seeing their children get dirty hands doing factory work. The idea has never surfaced again, not even under Gorbachev.

Brezhnev's years brought another leap forward in favor of social stability—or stagnation, depending on one's point of view. A kind of managerial tenure system developed, something Gor-bachev is trying to correct against a great deal of bureaucratic resistance.

Gorbachev inherited a society whose social mobility is no longer higher than in advanced capitalist countries, and may be even lower than in the United States. The result is the self-perpetuation of the managerial class, with some middle-class upward mobility, and less opportunity for advancement for those from worker or peasant backgrounds.

Stalin's purges in the 1930s, whatever their other conse-quences, did promote, in their very peculiar way, a great deal of social mobility by constantly emptying managerial chairs. After Khrushchev's 1956 denunciation of Stalin's methods, party cad-res were no longer subjected to such hazards. The purges taking place under Gorbachev are different in nature: they are aimed at the corrupt and the incompetent and, except for criminal cases, shift the purged person to a lesser job, not to a prison cell.

Education, connections, and money are the three components of social mobility in the West. In the Soviet Union, the first two apply in almost the same manner as in the West, but the third differs. Money plays a role: we read enough about bribed admissions to universities or the importance of private tutors to prepare for entrance exams. But money's influence is still much more limited than in the West, where papa's stock portfolio may put his son on the corporation's board of directors. Since money plays a lesser role, the third important element in Soviet social mobility is the party card. It must be said that a party card alone is no longer enough to open doors, but it can still tilt the scale given the proper education and connections.

The Standard of Living

15

Education

Of all the Soviet achievements, educational gains are the most impressive. The October revolution failed in many respects, but certainly not in the field of education. While prerevolutionary Russia was predominantly illiterate (72 percent in 1913), today's Soviet Union is overwhelmingly literate, with total illiterates ranging between 1 and 3 percent of the population. There are still a number of semi-literates, those able to read headlines and store signs only, but the latter are probably no more numerous than in the United States. An almost similar degree of literacy has been achieved in such areas as Soviet Central Asia, where prerevolutionary figures were even lower than those in Russia proper.

Education became the main vehicle of social advancement, as or more important than a party card and connections. The growth of education came in several stages. In the 1920s the emphasis was twofold: eradication of illiteracy and the creation of working-class elites. The former necessitated a mass effort to reach the largest possible number of people, whether in the cities or in the countryside, and educating them at least to the level of semi-literacy. The latter involved recruiting young workers with incomplete schooling for newly created technical institutes. There, a sound technical education was provided, although other subject matters were neglected, except for political indoctrination. The mission of these new *rabfaki* (workers' faculties) was to create new Soviet technical cadres, lacking, perhaps, the polish of the traditional intelligentsia, but compensating for any such deficiencies with devotion to the cause of building socialism.

The creation of workers' faculties, the priorities given to children of workers and peasants in entering regular universities, and the barring of the children of former nobles, officers, merchants, and bureaucrats from higher education, were all aimed at establishing a new Soviet intelligentsia radically different from its predecessor.

The 1920s also witnessed a number of educational experiments, ranging from complete student self-governance at the high school level to optional attendance of classes and free choice of curriculum. All such novelties were subsequently abandoned due to their failure to promote proper education. Restrictions based on discredited social origins were also discarded in the 1930s: the talent of the old intelligentsia was needed for economic advancement, especially in the five-year plans.

The Soviet educational system was consolidated during the 1930s and, with some minor changes, has retained the same basic structure to this day. The entire system is free, and has been so except for a short time from the end of World War II to Stalin's death. Students in institutions of higher learning are provided with stipends roughly on a par with minimum pension or minimum wage levels.

Exams are given at the end of each year, starting with the last year of primary school. Those who fail have to repeat the year. Grading in schools is done on a descending scale of 5 (A) to 1 (F). At the end of high school, there is a national examination, based on centrally prepared texts, similar to the French *baccalaureat* exam. Those who succeed receive "certificates of maturity," with or without a medal. The medals (gold or silver) correspond to our "*cum laude*" and "*magna cum laude*" distinctions.

The transition from high school to higher education is not automatic: entrance examinations are given to all applicants, with some priority reserved for those with silver or gold medals. The difficulty of the entrance examinations depends on the prestige of the institution. Thus to enter Moscow University is much more difficult than to enter an institute in Rostov-on-the-Don. Some institutions have even more restrictive admission policies. Thus the prestigious Institute of Foreign Relations selects not only the academically brilliant but the politically most reliable, the most strongly supported by party organizations, and the most highly recommended by well-connected officials.

Prior to World War II, compulsory education was limited to seven years in the cities and four in the countryside; now both have been increased to eight. The school year is long by our standards; six days per week, five to six classes per day, with a heavy emphasis on Russian and science courses. All subjects are compulsory, except for a choice of foreign languages (if more than one is offered by the given school). Similarly, the curriculum of higher education during the first two years is predetermined with a limited choice afterward (more restrictive than our "core curriculum"). Both school and university attendance is strictly monitored. Order in the classrooms is enforced, and nothing similar to American big cities' "blackboard jungle" can even be conceived.

Special schools exist for both gifted and retarded children. There are also boarding schools and elite schools with English (or French) as the language of instruction. Such schools are considered prestigious, and admission is highly competitive.

The system of education in the national republics follows the Russian pattern. But there schools are divided according to the language of instruction—that is, into national-language and Russian-language schools. Usually, all ten grades are covered in the schools taught in the principal language of the republic, but the languages of smaller ethnic groups are often taught only in primary grades. To continue, students must then shift to a school where the main language of instruction is the principal language of the republic, or Russian.

The problem of national schools is a very touchy one. Thus in the Ukraine one hears complaints about the demise of Ukrainian instruction in favor of Russian instruction. In Belorussia the language situation is even worse: native-language education has practically disappeared. In Azerbaijan, one hears complaints

The Soviet Education System

I. Preschool system

   1. Nurseries (ages 1–3)
   2. Kindergartens (ages 3–6)

II. School system

   1. Primary school (*nachal'naia shkola*), grades 1–3
   2. Junior high school (*nepolnaia sredniaia shkola*), grades 4–8.
   3. High school (*sredniaia shkola*), grades 9–10 (9–11 in some republics)

III. Technical education system

   1. Trade school (corresponding to grades 9–10 of high school)
   2. *Tekhnikum* (corresponding to trade school plus the junior college level—3–4 years of study)

IV. Higher education

   1. Institutes (medicine, engineering, etc.)
   2. Universities (4–5 year programs)

   The four levels of achievement in higher education:

   1. Student (undergraduate) level, first 4–5 years
   2. Aspirant (graduate student) level
   3. Candidate degree (first graduate degree, somewhere between our M.A. and Ph.D.)
   4. Doctor's degree (higher than our Ph.D., corresponding to the French *doctorat d'état* or the German *Doktor habil*).

from the smaller national minorities about the substitution of Azeri education for their own, and so forth.

The teaching of Russian in national schools, and of national languages in Russian schools, is another difficult issue. The teaching of Russian receives high priority for obvious reasons. But national-language instruction is very often taken lightly by Russian students. As a result, most Russian students living outside the Russian republic, from Uzbekistan to Estonia, fail to master the local language and remain estranged from the native population, something that does not help to improve national relations.

Another peculiarity of Soviet education is the presence of numerous evening and correspondence schools aimed at facilitating day-time employment while studying. The problem with evening and correspondence schools is their generally low standard, a situation very similar to that in the United States. Despite the absence of private education in the USSR, the gradation by prestige of educational institutions is similar in both countries. The best Soviet universities are the select institutions in Moscow and Leningrad, followed by prestigious schools in the Baltic republics and the Ukraine. Next come places of lesser prestige in the same locations and principal schools in the capitals of the larger union republics. In the last place are institutions located in regional centers. Thus, after the leading State University in Moscow come those in Leningrad, Kiev, Vilnius, and Tartu. At the bottom of the scale are such places as the Managerial Institute in Baku (closed for corruption not long ago), local teachers colleges, and correspondence institutions.

The basic structure of Soviet education has roots in the pre-revolutionary system, which in turn borrowed heavily from Western Europe, especially Germany. But the most important German implant was the Academy of Sciences, something unknown in the Anglo-Saxon world and existing elsewhere on a much more modest scale. The first Academy was established by Peter the Great in

Academy of Sciences Professional Staffs, 1987

	Academy of Sciences USSR (Moscow)	Academies of the Union Republics
Academicians (full and corresponding members)	932	1,428
Staff members with advanced degrees	33,922	29,748
Staff members without advanced degrees	61,452	56,659

Source: *Vestnik Statistiki*, 1988, no. 7, p. 67.

1724 in St. Petersburg and staffed by German scholars who could not speak Russian. Transferred to Moscow in 1924, it grew into an enormous body, spread to all the republics, and now employs hundreds of thousands of people, ranging from scholars to janitors. The Academy of Science system has a quasi-monopoly on Soviet research, and offers no teaching, though it accepts graduate degree candidates doing supervised work under its roof.

This neat division between research and teaching, with the bulk of research conducted in the Academy and teaching as well as some research in the universities, is the prevailing rule of Soviet scholarship. It is only lately, under Gorbachev, that the value of such a division of responsibilities has been questioned. Is it worth keeping such an enormous and costly research establishment, while in the West the universities assume the main burden and do it no worse than the Academy does in the USSR? Indeed, the number of Academy personnel is very large; over 30,000 in Moscow alone, not including support staff. Counting the latter, we come to even more impressive figures; the small republic of Armenia has 17,000 on its Academy payroll. The Institute of History of Azerbaijan alone employs 400 persons. These numbers include (nonteaching) professors, senior scientific workers, scientific workers, junior scientific workers, aides, secretaries, drivers, and janitors. In Moscow every seventh person is directly or indirectly connected with a research or educational establishment.

There is no doubt that some of the research warrants support. But whether this work requires such a large nonteaching staff is another matter. In private conversations many members of the Academy express the opinion that the majority of the staff could be dismissed without diminishing the scholarly output of the institution in question. However, the academies serve not only an academic role but a social one as well; they provide employment for scores of holders of graduate degrees who would otherwise have difficulty finding a job that corresponds to their qualifications.

16

Health Care

Another of the Soviet regime's proudest achievements is the national health-care system. Both universal and free, it covers the totality of the Soviet Union, from Moscow to the remotest district in Siberia. It shows a ratio of physicians and hospital beds practically unequaled in the world and superior to that of Western Europe or the United States (1 physician for every 220 inhabitants, roughly double the U.S. average). The system takes care of all citizens from cradle to grave and dispenses that care without charge. But at the same time, it is laden with an array of problems closely related to the very nature of ''socialized medicine.''

At its establishment, the Soviet health system was one of a kind. It contributed to the development of other universal free care systems, such as those that now exist in Western Europe, by offering the only operational model that could be imitated. But it differs from its Western counterparts in important ways.

First of all, except for a few specialists who are allowed to receive private patients after working hours, all Soviet health personnel work for the state. All hospitals, clinics, and dispensaries are state-run. Physicians are paid monthly wages, regardless of the number of patients treated. The English system of socialized medicine, which in many ways resembles the Soviet model, differs in that it is not a monopoly, and participating physicians are paid on the basis of the numbers of patients registered with them.

Another peculiarity of Soviet medicine was inherited from

prerevolutionary times: only a minority of Soviet physicians are M.D.s. The great majority have only physician's diplomas, not doctorates. The M.D. title is reserved mostly for specialists and not for general practitioners. This distinction is unknown in the West, where all licensed physicians, regardless of specialty, are required to have M.D. credentials. Similarly, all dentists are not D.D.S.s. Dentistry is also socialized and its services (but not the materials used) are free.

Unlike in England or in France, pharmaceuticals are not covered and have to be paid for by the patients. But drug prices are so low that this is not a great burden, even for the poor, and war veterans pay only half-price.

The problem with the system is not quantity but quality, something that was not much discussed in the Soviet press before Gorbachev but is now openly debated. Here are the main problems:

• Clinical facilities are, with few exceptions, well below Western standards. The waiting time in the reception areas is like that in our most crowded HMOs or emergency rooms, and the consultation is often brief and superficial.

• Previously backward areas of the country are now provided with doctors and hospitals, but the reality is less than rosy. The Soviet press reported that in the Turkmen republic, over 60 percent of maternity clinics and children's wards have no hot water, while 127 hospitals (roughly 40 percent of the total) lack running water altogether, and two-thirds have no sewers (modern cesspools are unknown there). All this despite statistical achievements: the number of physicians per capita in Turkmenistan is only 25 percent below the USSR average—and exceeds the U.S. average!

• The situation in Turkmenistan may show Soviet medicine at its worst; but even the much better institutions located in the European part of the USSR lag behind their Western counterparts. Wards are standard, equipment is outdated, and sanitary conditions are not on a par with ours.

Voices

". . . our country is still strongly affected by 'medical paternalism,' which has its roots in the time when the man in the white coat worked among an ignorant, illiterate population that did not know the first thing about hygiene. . . . But this kind of paternalism is out of date today. The population is much more sophisticated about general and health matters, is better informed, and has a better understanding of the interests of its own health and its right to protect its health. Consequently it was inevitable that there would be increased dissatisfaction over the present state of affairs. . . . People must participate in discussions on the siting of production facilities that present a potential hazard to health or on the introduction of hazard-free technologies, they must have the right to choose their physician or hospital, to obtain a second diagnosis, to monitor the course of introduction of a new medication or mode of therapy."

A. G. Vishnevskii in *Kommunist*, 1988, no. 6

• The element of choice is lacking. A patient is assigned to the first available physician. Access to the physician one prefers may require good connections and a willingness to pay.

• Salaries in the medical professions are low, on par with those of teachers. Only specialists with doctoral degrees and those teaching in medical institutes are well compensated. The average general practitioner is a woman and not highly paid. Women account for three out of every four physicians, and a higher proportion among nurses, nurse's aides, and *feldshery*—paramedical practitioners allowed to treat uncomplicated cases.

• While drugs are very cheap, many are hard to find, even if one has "connections" at the pharmacy. The same holds true for dental supplies: to avoid getting an aluminum crown or a steel tooth, one has to pay the dentist for quality material. Porcelain, apparently, is unavailable.

Low salaries, a shortage of adequate facilities, and a cumbersome bureaucracy create a situation propitious to open extortion. Everyone must be paid off. The aide, the nurse, the physician, and the dentist have to be paid under the table if the necessary work is to be honestly performed. The average "tariffs" are no secret; indeed, they were spelled out in an article in *Moscow News*: one ruble to the maid who changes the bed, five to the nurse who dispenses the medicine, ten to the doctor, and so forth. The total "gray income" in the medical profession is estimated by Soviet economists at 2–3 billion rubles, as compared with the total socialized medicine budget of 19 billion rubles (about 5 percent of the U.S. health budget).

Given the privileges granted to scores of influential *apparatchiki*, it would indeed be strange if the health system were exempt. And it is not. Special hospitals and pharmacies serve the privileged, places inaccessible to common mortals. And even these special facilities are not uniform; they are graded according to the degree of privilege extended to their patients. For example, the so-called Kremlin pharmacy, which serves selected high-ranking Muscovites, is better supplied than other select pharmacies open to lesser officials; and it goes without saying that it is much better supplied than the average pharmacy catering to the general public.

The system of sanatoriums is also multileveled, based on privilege. Well-equipped, secluded establishments in choice localities serve the most privileged, while poorly equipped, crowded places located in less desirable areas house the common crowd.

At present, discussions are under way in the Soviet press about a possible reform of the health care system. Reformers deplore the poor quality of health care, the lack of choice, and the unsatisfactory longevity data (Soviet life expectancy is below U.S. and Western European levels, and the child mortality rate ranks thirty-fourth in the world), despite the saturation of the system with doctors and hospital beds. What is being envisaged is a partially contributory system (except for the poor) that allows for a greater

Voices

"The southern shore of the Crimea has become a very undemocratic place in our days. Most of the attractive and accessible seashore parcels have already been allocated to fashionable sanatoriums for officialdom—and fenced in. The number and length of beaches open to the general public is small and not growing at all."

From a letter to *Komsomol'skaia pravda*, August 28, 1988

choice of physicians and medical facilities.

It is too early to predict what exactly will take place, but one can anticipate the establishment of nominal fees to discourage unwarranted overutilization of services, and some paying free-choice alternatives for those who can and do choose to pay more for special care. This will not be easy to achieve given the ideological commitment to free and equal access to medicine. But since privilege through position or connections already exists, and it is common knowledge that bribes are being given (and taken) by almost everybody, reforms may eventually have a chance.

Despite its obvious shortcomings, Soviet medicine has indisputably accomplished its main task: it has provided the country with a universal, freely accessible health system and lifted Soviet health standards almost to the level of other advanced industrial nations.

17

Housing

In the large cities of the USSR, housing is predominantly public, with some cooperative units and only a very few remaining privately owned single-family houses. The smaller the city, the higher the proportion of private houses. In the countryside private housing prevails.

Public housing is heavily subsidized and rents are set way below the cost of maintenance, without even taking into consideration the amortization of construction costs. By contrast, the owners of cooperative apartments not only pay the cost of construction (or at least a part of it), but their monthly maintenance is several times that of rentals.

Obviously, with rents so low and the housing shortage acute, getting a rental apartment is very difficult. Basically, there are two ways: through the city housing administration and through the place of employment. The latter may have an allocation of apartments in public houses under construction (or planned), or the right to an entire building for the exclusive use of its personnel.

The problem is that the waiting lists for housing are so long that it can take many years before one's application reaches the top of the pile. Thus all possible connections are explored, all imaginable priorities claimed, and all necessary bribes disbursed. The goal is to move oneself to the head of the list, bypassing the less well connected and the less fortunate.

A good proportion of Soviet urban dwellers still live in communal apartments shared by several unrelated persons or even families. Others have to live in workers' dormitories, furnished with bunks, or sublet accommodations in private homes at rents ten times those charged by the state.

The amount of communal and dorm housing is difficult to judge. In Moscow it supposedly accounts for 20 percent of all housing. This is an improvement over conditions thirty years ago, when such dwellings were clearly in the majority. Workers' dormitories are mostly inhabited by young bachelors, but it is not unknown for newlyweds to live in dormitories, even when a child is born. Private rentals are not always available and are often very selective (no children, no pets) and expensive.

For the luckiest tenants of public houses, the main problem is upkeep and repairs. As mentioned, rents cover little, and maintenance funds are limited. In addition, spare parts are scarce, and paints, building material, wallpaper, and the like are difficult to obtain.

The waiting time between a request for repairs and the arrival of a repairman is long and can only be shortened by connections or money, often by a combination of both. And when the repairman finally arrives, the tenant pays "under the table" to avoid a sloppy job.

The litany of complaints in this field is endless, inspiring a number of jokes on the subject. Still, given the low rents, a Soviet citizen who has managed to install himself and his family in a decent publicly owned apartment has even more rights and advantages than the proverbial rent-controlled New Yorker: the Soviet citizen is living practically rent-free, at the cost of poor maintenance.

Cooperative apartments account for a small proportion of the total and, again, are not exactly patterned on ours. They are purchased at a specific price, on the average between 10,000 and 20,000 rubles, and maintenance is generally in the vicinity of 40 or 50 rubles per month. As in other countries, co-ops can be sold at a profit at market prices. But here the similarities end. First of all, these apartments cannot be bought by just anyone, but only by

Voices

"Most of the 'ways' [of getting an apartment] are well known. They are based on the certitude that ranks and positions give special rights; not only to rank-holders, but to their children as well. None of our 'restructurings' have shaken this belief. During working hours they love to talk about *perestroika*. But after working hours they write letters, or more often make telephone calls, with requests (or are they demands?) for two- or three-room or even larger apartments for their newly married offspring. And not just anywhere, but in the center of the capital, and in a well-constructed building. Certainly as an exception, since their child is not on any waiting list, and is not inclined to get on one. . . ."

From a discussion in *Nedelia*, 1987, No. 25

This year three-room apartments will be allocated to Muscovites who have been on the waiting list since 1978–79 . . . except for those with priorities. . . .

From *Vecherniaia Moskva*, July 22, 1987

those who have the right to do so, since co-ops are generally built for employees of a certain sector (a union, a ministry, an enterprise, etc.), and outsiders do not qualify. Thus money is not the only prerequisite for buying into the co-op. The advantage of the co-op as against a rental is the possibility of having a larger and better-constructed apartment and getting it much sooner than one would by waiting in line for a rental.

Another type of lodging either belongs or is assigned to a given enterprise. This housing may be used as bait to attract and keep qualified employees, since the latter would lose their lodgings if they left the job.

Voices

In room No. 640 a family occupies a bunkbed. Let's be precise: each family. There are two of them. In fourteen square meters: three toddlers, four adults. The toddlers sleep with their mothers, since there is no place for cots—no place to put them, and it is not allowed: the dormitory is for singles, and there is only bunk space. . . .

. . . It's most difficult when the husband is not around. Sure, at this moment he is there, alongside. But only until 11 p.m. After that, he has to leave . . . [Otherwise] he will be fined for violating police registration rules. . . .

A conversation transcribed during the management's memorable visit to the dormitory:

VOICE: "My name is Baiburina, a machine operator at the factory since 1972. I lived in the dormitory. Then I got married, was renting privately. A child was born. Even if you offer 70 rubles [per month], they chase you out. Got accepted into the dormitory with the child, but they said they wouldn't give us a [police] residence permit because my husband works in a different factory.

I went everywhere, nobody even wanted to listen. What should we do—get a divorce? Tell me, do I have a right to a lodging or not?"

SOROKIN [factory deputy director]: "Like all Soviet citizens, you do, according to the Constitution. But to have it, you have to get it."

BAIBURINA: "Don't I merit it after fifteen years?"

SOROKIN: "But you are living [here]."

BAIBURINA: "But I live here illegally."

SOROKIN: "You are not allowed to live here illegally."

BAIBURINA: "Then make it legal! And then, what to do with the child, when I work two shifts? They don't let my husband in after 11 at night."

SOROKIN: "Then your husband shouldn't work."

BAIBURINA: "My husband lives in the Soviet Union, he is not a parasite."

From *Komsomol'skaia pravda*, September 22, 1987

Individual houses still exist in many Soviet cities. They remain privately owned and vary greatly in quality and size. They can be quite large and comfortable or ramshackle and decrepit. The most comfortable ones might cost a hundred thousand rubles or more. Others are "illegal" dwellings, constructed with no permit and no basic amenities. A great deal depends on the location, the owner's status, the period when the house was built, and so forth. A private home might be a Finnish-style structure built by an Estonian writer or a slum dwelling in a suburb of Tashkent.

By recent accounts, in Tashkent alone (a city of about 2 million inhabitants), single-family houses built without permits and with few amenities number 32,000 and provide shelter not only for their owners but for over 11,000 students who fail to get into regular dormitories. The same city also still has a number of traditionally built one-family homes with interior courtyards and modern amenities, which have not yet been absorbed by the expansion of modern lookalike cement housing blocks.

There is another element in the Soviet housing picture, one with no parallel outside the Soviet bloc: the problem of police registration, or *propiska*. Not that police registration is something unusual: many European countries still enforce it. But in Western Europe this practice amounts to registration pure and simple, whereas in the USSR registration means permission to reside. Such permission is very difficult to obtain in the capital and in other desirable cities. It requires strong support from one's employer, the ability to get a place to live (a Sisyphean effort by itself), a lot of perseverance, some good connections, and a willingness to "oil" the machinery whenever necessary.

There have been cases of musicians accepting building handyman jobs in Moscow in order to secure an abode, then bribing their way to a *propiska*. In Tallin some Russian immigrants from the impoverished areas around Pskov or Novgorod arrive alone, accept hard-to-fill manual-labor jobs in heavy industry, secure a bunk in a workers' dormitory, all in order to get the desired *propiska*. Eventually, they bring their families in, look for better lodging, and change jobs, thus leaving the labor-hungry factory hunting for new workhands.

An apartment in Moscow makes a single woman very desirable in the eyes of a provincial bachelor planning his move to the capital. Reportedly there have even been cases of people taking an orphan for adoption in order to be granted a better lodging on that basis, then returning the child to the orphanage as too difficult to handle!

Exchanges of apartments are a big business. Ads proliferate in local papers, in special publications, on walls, and on tree trunks.

As far as the appearance and quality of Soviet apartments is concerned, this varies according to the period of construction. Housing construction was largely neglected during Stalin's era. Priority was given to industrial plants, public buildings, and monumental "wedding cake" highrises. Faced with a tremendous housing crisis, Khrushchev attempted to remedy the situation by massive construction of poor quality cement-block houses. The housing stock grew rapidly, but twenty years later these buildings are in poor condition inside and out. Aggravating the general problem of poor construction and maintenance is the widespread incidence of theft of building materials from construction sites.

A foreigner visiting a Moscow apartment building is generally taken aback by the bleakness of narrow, utilitarian entrance halls. Common areas—corridors, staircases, elevators, etc.—look neglected. Everything that can rust, rusts; what can chip, chips; what can crack, cracks. But inside, the apartments are often decent. Sanitary and kitchen equipment is in place, though there are no dishwashers, microwave ovens, or food processors. Furniture is outmoded by our standards, but passable. Co-operative apartments look a notch better and are larger as well.

The devastating earthquake that shook Soviet Armenia in December 1988, destroying several towns, put an international spotlight on shoddy Soviet construction practices. Foreign rescue workers searching for survivors in the rubble of multistoried buildings were outspoken in their criticisms of the design, inferior building materials, and poor quality of construction, which they believed contributed to the heavy loss of life. Theft and corruption are said to play no small part in the problem. A government investigation of the construction industry was promised, and construction standards are now certain to be raised.

The government has pledged that by the year 2000 every Soviet family will have a single-family house or an individual apartment. Communal or dormitory accommodations will be the exception, for young bachelors studying or learning a trade. But to solve the housing problem by the year 2000 will necessitate an enormous effort (Moscow alone builds 530,000 square meters per year of new living space), and the older housing stock continues to decay rapidly. Even if the program succeeds, it will probably fall short of giving every citizen the minimal 9 square meters (100 square feet) of living space to which he is legally entitled.

18

Prices and Wages

The Soviet system of prices and wages contrasts sharply with a capitalist system in which almost everything is determined by market conditions of supply and demand, notwithstanding governmental regulations and taxation policies.

In the Soviet Union the price of an item is set in Moscow, taking into account the cost of production, social need, and political advantage, with the last two considerations often prevailing over the first. Thus, essential goods—including basic housing, food staples, public transportation, medicine, publications, and popular entertainment—are priced way below cost.

At the same time, items seen as luxuries—cars, appliances, alcoholic beverages, cosmetics, and so on—are heavily taxed and priced way above their actual cost. Basic items of clothing remain relatively expensive, but better clothing, associated with luxury, is greatly overtaxed.

The mechanism used for manipulating prices is a combination of subsidies and taxes, especially the turnover tax. An extreme example is the price of meat, which is sold in state stores at about one-third of production cost, whereas cars are priced way above their actual cost. Similarly, rents not only do not cover construction costs but fail to cover maintenance as well, so it is no surprise that the heavily subsidized housing stock is in a constant state of disrepair. In the meantime, a private individual with a spare room can rent it to a desperate tenant (a not exactly legal but widespread occurrence) for many times the official ''price'' of apartment rental—a reflection of the reality of supply and demand.

116

**Soviet and American Family Budgets
(basic expenses, in %)**

	USA	USSR
Food	14.8	28.3
Clothing	5.1	15.0
Housing	30.3	10.0
Other expenses	49.8	46.7

Notes: The 10 percent figure for housing in the USSR is an estimate. In the Soviet source the housing budget (rents and utilities) is lumped with services, for a total of 23.8 percent of total expenses. Also, the Soviet food budget figure excludes alcoholic beverages, which are said to amount to as much as 20 percent of the family budget. Another Soviet source gives family budget figures of 36.4 percent for food and 16.6 percent for alcohol.

Sources: For the United States, Bureau of Labor Statistics data reported in *The New York Times,* October 26, 1988. For the USSR, a survey of over 60,000 families, reported in *Komsomol'skaia pravda,* August 24, 1988.

Constant shortages as well as the presence of several pricing systems complicate the matter even further. There are, after all, not only state stores but kolkhoz "farmers'" markets for food-stuffs, a "black market" for consumer goods, a "gray market" for services, special stores with limited access, stores that only accept special coupons, "hard currency" stores, and so on. How can one possibly determine the "real" price of a kilo of apples of a certain variety if the state store has only rotten apples, the kolkhoz market shows several prices, and special stores have their own array of prices, depending on the classification of their clientele?

This confusion of prices and uncertainty of supply makes it very difficult to evaluate the Soviet cost of living. The wide range of prices for goods sold in kolkhoz markets located in different regions adds new complications. The availability of fixed-price products in state stores also varies drastically, with Moscow being privileged and remote towns poorly supplied. On the other hand, a small town located in the southern belt (Central Asia, Transcaucasia, Moldavia, Ukraine) or in one of the Baltic republics will generally have a decent kolkhoz market, able to compensate for shortages in state food stores, but at higher prices. Moscow, on

Average Prices of Agricultural Products Sold at Urban Farmers' Markets in 264 Cities (rubles and kopecks per kilo)

Item	July 1985	July 1987	January 1988	State prices (Moscow) 1987	1988
Potatoes	.44	.55	.71	.10	
Fresh cabbage	.61	.86	.71	.20	
Onions	1.01	.90	.63	.70	.50
Green onions	1.79	1.33	3.08	.50	
Fresh carrots	1.08	1.16	.70	.10	.15
Fresh cucumbers	1.42	1.60	6.31	.60	3.00
Fresh tomatoes	1.80	2.38	5.61	1.00	2.00
Garlic	3.00	3.20	3.77	2.00	
Apples	2.17	2.62	2.36	.80	1.50
Beef	4.91	4.95	5.01	2.00	
Lamb	5.15	5.15	5.05	1.90	
Pork	4.38	4.47	4.59	2.10	
Lard	3.92	3.94	4.22	2.40	
Butter	7.42	7.91	8.16	3.60	

Source: USSR State Statistical Committee data as reported in Sotsiologicheskie issledovaniia, 1987, No. 5, p. 131, and 1988, No. 3, p. 23.

the other hand, although provided with better supplied state stores, has very high prices at kolkhoz markets, sometimes several times higher than those of the southern belt, especially for fruits and vegetables.

We are thus faced with the following variety of prices. For foodstuffs there are state prices, with minor regional variations. Then there are kolkhoz market prices, with important regional variations. And within the kolkhoz market there are two sets of prices: those charged by kolkhoz and sovkhoz stands, which sell farm surpluses, and the even higher prices demanded by individuals selling products from their own private garden plots. Finally, there are the food prices charged by closed distributors of every kind, which are usually set at or below state prices, and provide better quality goods.

Voices

"Almost everywhere . . . there are two trading systems and two service systems: one open to everyone, the other for 'our people.' According to sociological investigations 83 percent of the population overpays for goods and services (in one form or another, everyone has 'their own' butcher, 'their own' barber, a connection for shoes, etc.).

. . . An effective solution to the problems of the black market can be achieved only through the liquidation of the objective causes, built into the economic system."

G. Belikova and A. Shokhin in *Ogonek*, September 1987

For manufactured goods, in addition to state stores and closed distributors, the "black market" comes into play as well. Here sellers are many: there are those who managed to buy a *defitsit* (short-supply item) at the state store and want to resell it; those who have returned from a trip abroad and are trying to recover their expenses (or simply make money) by selling a few foreign products; and finally, professional black-marketeers who move large quantities of goods and take great risks in doing so, bribing officials to look the other way.

Black market transactions can take place anywhere, from the back doors of state stores to kolkhoz markets, from second-hand car markets to private apartments. State offices are not excluded. Prices show great variety, depending on availability and risk, with the seller often "doing a favor" for the eager customer, who is willing to pay any price for an otherwise unobtainable item.

But the largest of Soviet "gray markets" is probably the one for services. According to recent Soviet data, the yearly volume of this gray market is somewhere between 16 billion and 18 billion rubles, as against 9.8 billion for state-supplied services.

**"Unofficial Services" as Share of Total Services
(USSR as a whole)**

Apartment repairs	45%
Car repairs	40%
Household items repair	30%

Pravda, September 5, 1987

Needs of car owners covered by state trade	15–20%

Izvestiia, August 4, 1987

Share of Private and Garden Plots in Total Agriculture

Share of arable land:	2.7%
Share of agricultural production	est. 25%

Izvestiia, June 9, 1987

The number of retired pensioners and persons employed by a state enterprise who work "on the side" in the service sector may reach 18 million. Moreover, virtually all of the 35 million families working on kolkhozes market their private plot products. Considering that the total Soviet labor force is somewhere around 120 million, this means that every third, or even every second, person is taking part in some private activity.

Within the gray market for services, a prominent place is occupied by the private car-repair business. State shops manage to perform only a fraction of needed repairs. Another massive sector is the apartment repair and maintenance business. Electronics and appliance repair, private tutoring, tailoring, and household help come next.

Recent Soviet legislation makes it easier for people with initiative to register themselves and offer such services openly, once they pay the proper taxes and license fees. But this seemingly desirable change has encountered some resistance because many prefer to work "undeclared" in order to avoid all control and taxation.

Actual Soviet personal incomes are not easy to determine and even more difficult to translate into figures that make sense to Western readers. Translating rubles into dollars means little: the official exchange rate for one ruble is $1.65; but black marketeers pay five rubles for a dollar in Moscow and more in the provinces. Soviet currency is not officially convertible. The fact that numerous goods and services are either subsidized or overtaxed, and that prices vary depending on the distributor (state store, kolkhoz markets, black markets, special distributors), further complicates efforts to determine the cost of living. Besides, the availability of everything is uncertain and depends on access and privilege as much as on money. Moreover, many people on low salaries are in a position to supplement their incomes through after-hours work, speculation, or tolerated theft.

Under such circumstances, how can one make sensible comparisons between the incomes of two individuals, one of whom has better access to housing and closed distributors, the other more ways to supplement his income by legal, illegal, or semilegal means?

Still, there is no way to avoid discussing official salaries, even while taking all possible "ifs" and "buts" into consideration. In this context, two additional peculiarities should be kept in mind. The first is that wide salary spreads were traditionally considered unsocialist, and as a result, the range was kept narrower than economically justified. The second is that, except for some liberal professions (writers, artists) and for private plot owners, all legal income in the USSR comes from wages.

How great are the salary differences? The top level is about 2,000 rubles as against 60 rubles per month at the bottom. The lowest salary corresponds to that of a cleaning lady in a rural office, the top represents the compensation of a full member of the Academy of Sciences of the USSR—someone of Andrei Sakharov's stature.

Best- and Worst-paid Occupations in the USSR (1 = best)

	1983	1960	1940
Construction	1	2	4
Transportation	2	4	5
Industry	3	3	6
Science	4	1	1
Banking and insurance	5	7	7
Agriculture	6	13	13
Management	7	5	3
Communications	8	9	9
Trade	9	11	12
Housing and services	10	12	10
Education	11	6	8
Art	12	8	2
Health	13	10	11
Culture	14	14	14

Source: S. L. Osipov, *Zarabotnaia plata: proportsii, dinamika, tendentsii* (Vladivostok, 1986).

But these figures are misleading. Closer to reality would be the 80–800 ruble range. The latter can be divided as follows: 80–120 rubles per month for low-paying jobs; 120–180 rubles for average ones; 180–240 rubles in the better-paid occupations; 240–400 rubles in managerial positions; and 400–800 rubles per month for top executives, scholars, and ranking military officers. A district party first secretary receives 540 rubles per month.

Statistically, the average Soviet monthly pay is placed around 200 rubles per month, but the prevailing median seems closer to 160 rubles, with an average of 10 percent deducted for taxes. This is what physicians, teachers, lawyers, librarians, and a score of other middle-level professionals earn. Similarly, engineers, whose average pay in 1940 was between 2.2 and 2.4 times higher than that of factory workers, lost their advantage, and are now making only about 10 percent more.

Legal and medical professionals, on average, are not among the best paid. Their salaries remain at the level of a high school teacher's. Of course, patients do tip their doctors on the side, thus increasing their real income. Soviet lawyers, who enter law school after high school, not after college, are primarily "in-house" lawyers, dealing with problems arising between state enterprises and not pleading in courts. Those who defend corrupt officials or speculators against criminal charges manage to earn high incomes. Soviet engineers, for their part, often perform jobs that in the United States are assigned to technicians.

The top of the Soviet salary structure is also unlike ours. Prominent scholars and writers, military officers from lieutenant colonels on up, and the managers of large enterprises receive high compensation. In the United States, only the last group occupies this place, along with top professionals and athletes.

If we compare our system of compensation with the Soviet system (urban occupations only), we get the following impressionistic picture of the two income structures.

	United States	**USSR**
Top:	businessmen	politicians
	executives	academicians
Upper:	lawyers	salesclerks
	doctors	military
	managers	executives
Medium:	politicians	managers
	scholars	skilled workers
	military	scholars
	writers	
Lower:	teachers	physicians
	engineers	unskilled workers
	skilled workers	teachers, lawyers
Bottom:	white-collar workers	white-collar workers
	salesclerks	unskilled and
	unskilled and	manual labor
	manual labor	

As one can see, only toward the bottom of the scale are the rows comparable. One also has to keep in mind that practically all Soviet managers, as well as those clerks who work in trade or services, make a good deal of money on the side, increasing their financial resources significantly.

With our tendency to view the Soviet Union as politically, economically, and socially uniform, often we not only simplify the social situation but picture the Soviet way of life in a regionally undifferentiated manner. Those who know the Soviet Union better succumb in turn to a different set of simplifications, influenced by the popular conceptions prevailing among the Soviet population. Thus, Moscow is perceived as the epitome of better living, the Transcaucasian republics as the home of wheeler-dealers, Central Asia as the mainstay of private initiative, provincial Russia as the most deprived region, and the Baltic republics as the most Westernized. On closer examination, some but not all of these preconceptions are confirmed.

The highest standards of living are to be found in the Baltic republics, especially in Estonia. In Transcaucasia, Georgia and Armenia are better off than Azerbaijan. All three of these republics are fertile grounds for moneymaking, but the disparity in incomes between those who manage to make it and those who don't is wide, so that average living standards are not so impressive. In short, while there is a great deal of money and corruption around, the average citizen is worse off than someone living in the Baltic republics.

Private initiative is alive and well in Central Asia and Transcaucasia. A great deal of this is due to climatic conditions, closer family ties, and a general dislike of factory work and discipline. Ukraine and southern Russia, with their fertile soil and "southern" disposition, do manage better than the northern areas.

Moscow's standards are also misleading since more than half of the inhabitants work for administrative or academic institutions. Privileges flourish there, closed distributors proliferate, foreigners are a source of imported goods, and, in general, Soviet

North-South Comparison of Living Standards
(Estonia, Georgia, and Azerbaijan 1985; Uzbekistan 1986)

	Estonia	Georgia	Azerbaijan	Uzbekistan
Population (in millions)	1.542	5.234	6.718	19.013
Average wage (rubles/mo.)	214.3	167	163.7	165.5
in industry	230.0	199.5	—	181.5
in agriculture	255.8	138.8	—	158.6
Housing space, sq. meters per capita				
cities	17.7	15.9	11.8	11.2
country	26.5	19.2	8.4	10.8
Durable goods per 1000 inhabitants				
television sets	349	240	193	159
refrigerators	394	244	171	145
private cars	109	n.a.	n.a.	n.a.
Food consumption per capita in kg. per year				
meat	89	45	35	31
fish	24.6	8.8	4.4	5
fruits, vegetables	79	81	71	107
bread/grain products	92	188	161	177

n.a. = not available.

Sources: *Narodnoe khoziaistvo Estonskoi SSR. Statisticheskii ezhegodnik, 1985*, Tallin, 1986; *Narodnoe khoziaistvo Gruzinskoi SSR v 1985 godu. Statisticheskii ezhegodnik*, Tbilisi, 1986; *Azerbaidzhan v tsifrakh v 1985 godu*, Baku, 1986; *Uzbekskaia SSR v tsifrakh 1986*, Tashkent, 1987.

trade authorities give high priority to Moscow's needs. But non-privileged Muscovites, who after all do exist, are worse off than their counterparts in the Baltic region, where the distribution system appears to be fairer and less dependent on privileges.

Our tables comparing regional living standards are based on official Soviet data for 1985 and 1986 (the latest available), but cannot be analyzed uncritically. Comparing monthly wages without taking into account the average family size underestimates the relative prosperity of regions with smaller families. Comparing available housing without taking into account climatic differences underestimates the conditions in warmer areas, where less inside space is needed. Food consumption must be seen in the light of both climatic conditions and traditional eating habits. Moreover, undeclared and unregistered earnings and consumption play an important role. Despite all these objections, however, the data from the four republics should be useful. The only alternative is to dispense with statistical measurements altogether.

19

The Demographic Picture

Demographic data can be extremely informative. Among other things, they tell us how many people are living where, whether they live among others of their own ethnic background or dispersed, or whether they live where they are "needed" in economic terms. We can learn which population groups are growing, which declining in size, and how these changes are linked to high or low birth rates, death rates, and life expectancies. Demographic data for the Soviet Union give us a revealing picture on all these counts.

The first complete Russian imperial census, taken in 1897, registered a total population of 126 million, out of which 42 percent were Russians, and 24 percent were Ukrainians ("Little Russians") and Belorussians. Muslims (outside the protectorates of Khiva and Bukhara) made up 11 percent, Poles over 6 percent, and Jews over 4 percent.

The first Soviet census of 1926, taken two years after Lenin's death, shows the Russians moving from 42 percent to 52 percent of the total population. Ukrainians, Belorussians, and Muslims maintained their old proportions, and Poles and Jews dropped respectively to 0.5 percent and 2 percent due to the reestablishment of the Polish state. The total population numbered 147 million, down from 159 million in 1913. The change in ethnic balances and low total increase reflects wartime loss of lives as well as the postrevolutionary border changes to the detriment of the new Soviet state: 23 million inhabitants, predominantly non-

Russians, found themselves outside of Soviet frontiers.

The 1937 Soviet census has never been published. It was shelved because the resulting figures would have shown heavy human losses directly attributable to the forced collectivization campaign of 1929–32, the massive deportations of "kulaks," and the ensuing famine.

According to the 1939 census, the population of the USSR had reached 170 million, with Russians accounting for 58 percent (the highest percentage in modern times), while Ukrainians and Belorussians dropped to under 20 percent, reflecting losses in the wake of collectivization, especially harsh in the Ukraine. The proportion of Muslims increased slightly, from 11 to 12 percent, their high birth rates neutralized by very heavy losses suffered by Kazakhs during collectivization.

The 1959 census reflects World War II territorial gains as well as human losses. First of all, the Soviet Union absorbed Lithuania, Latvia, Estonia, and Tanu Tuva in their totality, plus chunks of Finnish, Polish, German, Czechoslovak, Romanian, and Japanese territory, with a total 1939 population of 23.5 million, almost exactly compensating the USSR for post–World War I territorial losses. On the other hand, the country suffered heavy wartime casualties, nullifying those gains. The totality of Soviet war losses, direct and indirect, has never been precisely calculated. The figure of 20 million mentioned by Khrushchev seems arbitrary, with some Russian demographers mentioning the much higher figure of 50 million. This high figure is reached by including concentration camp deaths, losses suffered by "punished nationalities," Vlasov army casualties, as well as the indirect demographic consequences of wartime losses. The 1959 census registered a total population of 209 million, with Russians slightly down to 55 percent of the total, Ukrainians and Belorussians up to 22 percent, and Muslims remaining at 11 percent.

Two principal factors marked the country's demographic situation during the first half of the twentieth century. The first was urbanization, transforming a rural society with only 18 percent urban dwellers into an urban society with 66 percent urban dwellers in 1987 (the respective figures for Central Asia are 19 percent and 41 percent). The second factor was the initial ability of the Slavic population to absorb heavy losses while maintaining its demographic vitality. This capacity, however, has been shattered by an accumulated "fatigue," leading to the demographic deterioration of the Slavs during the second part of our century.

The recent period, marked by the censuses of 1959, 1970, and 1979, illustrates the new trend: Russian, Ukrainian, and Belorussian birth rates experienced rapid decline, whereas Muslim birth rates went down much more slowly than expected. A relative decline in Muslim child mortality played a role as well. Notwithstanding this, in 1986 the number of children who died before reaching the age of one was 46.2 per 1,000 in Uzbekistan as against 19.3 per 1,000 in the Russian federation. But no such great disparity characterizes longevity data: 63.8 years for men and 74 years for women in the RSFSR as against 65.1 years for men and 71 years for women in Uzbekistan, presumably reflecting the consequences of alcoholism among Russian men and the toll of childbirth among Uzbek women.

The 1970 census showed that children under fourteen accounted for 24–27 percent of the population among eastern Slavs, but 48–51 percent among the major Muslim groups. Moreover, between 1959 and 1970, numerical gains among the Slavic groups amounted to 9.4–14.4 percent, while among Muslim groups the respective figures varied from 46.3 to 52.9 percent.

The proportion of Russians within the USSR has moved down from 55 percent in 1959, to 53 percent in 1970, to 52 percent in 1979, and most probably fell below 50 percent by 1986. That of Ukrainians and Belorussians together remained around 20.5 percent, while Muslims increased their share to 14 percent in 1970 and 16 percent in 1979. But it is among children under ten that the trends are most striking. Thus, in 1979, Russian children accounted for only 46 percent of all children under ten, and Ukrainians and Belorussians for 19.5 percent, while Muslim children in that age group moved from 9 percent in 1959 to 18 percent in

Demographic Data

Population Growth and Urbanization	1913	1939	1959	1987
Total USSR population (in millions)	159	191	209	282
% urban	18	32	48	66

Share of Principal Ethnic Groups in Population (%)	1959	1979	2000 (proj.)
Russians	54	52	48
Ukrainians and Belorussians	21	19	17
Muslims of all nationalities	10	17	25
Others	15	12	10

Natural Population Growth per 1000	1965	1986
Russian SFSR	8.1	6.8
Uzbek SSR	28.8	30.8
Georgian SSR	14.2	9.9
Estonian SSR	4.1	4.0

Average Family Size, 1979 (ethnically homogeneous families)	
Russians, Ukrainians, Belorussians	3.2
Latvians, Estonians	3.0
Jews	2.9
Georgians	4.0
Uzbeks	6.2
Tajiks	6.5

1970 and 27 percent in 1979. And these data do not include Muslim groups living within the RSFSR (Tatars, Bashkirs, the peoples of the North Caucasus, and some smaller nationalities). If these groups are counted in, the Muslim figure could go over 30 percent. Projections for the year 2000 are even more challenging: almost every second child born in the USSR may be born of Muslim parents, creating a totally altered demographic picture for the country as a whole.

The latest Soviet data (1986) fail to give natural growth figures by nationality, supplying only figures per republic. Per 1,000 inhabitants, the figures were, respectively, 6.8 for the RSFSR, 4.4 for Ukraine, 30.8 for Uzbekistan, and 35.2 for Tajikistan, an excellent illustration of the contrasting Slavic and Muslim birth rates.

The demographic situation described above has created a new manpower supply reality in the country as a whole. With European cohorts barely able to replace retiring ones, a fresh supply of workers from the Muslim southern belt is the only labor reserve the country can count on. But the problem is complicated by the fact that oversupply of labor in one region does not necessarily compensate for shortages in another. The reasons are two, the first being that industrial concentration and the largest raw material riches of the country happen to be located outside of labor-surplus regions.

The second factor is that Muslim workers, even when faced with unemployment, are extremely reluctant to relocate to labor-hungry "Christian" regions. Religious, cultural, and linguistic factors play a dissuasive role, reinforced by the lack of genuine economic incentive to move. It is still easier to muddle through in the climatically pleasant south, favorable to private initiative and agriculturally rich, than to cope with endless food shortages and a harsh climate in the less hospitable north.

In any case, most of the emigrants leaving the south are European settlers (or settlers' sons and daughters) who found themselves in Central Asia or the Caucasus as a result of previous migrations (whether prerevolutionary treks, Stalin's deportations, or Khrushchev's "virgin land" schemes). This phenomenon, known as *obratnichestvo* (movement back), accounts for the bulk of northward migration. While economically justified, it lessens the European presence in the Muslim south, a presence already dwindling under the impact of high Muslim birth rates.

Population of the USSR by Republic

Republic	Population in millions (January 1987)	Net growth per 1000 (1986)
USSR	281.7	10.2
RSFSR	145.3	6.8
including:		
Bashkir ASSR	3.9	
Buriat ASSR	1.0	
Dagestan ASSR	1.8	
Kabarda-Balkar ASSR	0.7	
Kalmyk ASSR	0.3	
Karelian ASSR	0.8	
Komi ASSR	1.2	
Mari ASSR	0.7	
Mordva ASSR	1.0	
North Ossetia ASSR	0.6	
Tatar ASSR	3.6	
Tuva ASSR	0.3	
Udmurt ASSR	1.6	
Chechen-Ingush ASSR	1.3	
Yakut ASSR	1.0	
Ukraine	51.2	4.4
Belorussia	10.1	7.4
Uzbekistan	19.0	30.8
including:		
Kara-Kalpak ASSR	1.1	
Kazakhstan	16.2	18.1
Kirgizia	4.1	25.5
Tajikistan	4.8	35.2
Turkmenistan	3.4	28.5
Azerbaijan	6.8	20.9
including:		
Nakhichevan ASSR	0.3	
Georgia	5.3	9.9
including:		
Ajar ASSR	0.5	
Abkhaz ASSR	0.4	
Armenia	3.4	18.3
Lithuania	3.6	6.6
Latvia	2.6	4.0
Estonia	1.6	4.0
Moldavia	4.2	13.8

Source: *SSSR v tsifrakh. Statisticheskii ezhegodnik*, 1987.

It thus appears very unlikely that the manpower problems of the European USSR, and especially of Siberia, will be solved by a repetition of the sort of northward migration of labor that was characteristic in the capitalist West. Consequently, there is no alternative to increasing labor efficiency and improving agricultural productivity. These are precisely the goals Gorbachev proposes to accomplish by dismantling some of the legal and bureaucratic constraints on individual initiative in the USSR.

20

The Quality of Life

Quality of life is very difficult to translate into measurable terms. One can, however, discuss it on the basis of essential components: living space, cleanliness, pollution and noise control, access to necessary amenities (from supplies to recreation), green space, even the aesthetic value of architecture and of the urban landscape in general, including what the Germans call *Gemütlichkeit*, or pleasantness. Measured by these criteria, the Soviet way of life fares poorly on most accounts.

We think of Switzerland as a clean place to live, and of the slums in the South Bronx as exactly the opposite. Soviet cities are at neither extreme. They cannot possibly match New York's mountains of garbage (for lack of wrapping material and disposable containers). But marred building facades, mud puddles, cockroaches, rusting pipes, debris, and dirt are everywhere.

Regionally, the situation varies. The western borderlands and the more prosperous parts of the southern belt are in better shape, while the old industrial areas of Russia proper and the poorer parts of the south remain in substandard condition. Except in the western regions, public toilets are a disaster throughout the country. In Moscow's largest department store, the famous GUM, not only is the assortment of goods of lamentably poor quality, but the stench can lead the visitor straight to the men's room. Some prestigious academic institutions in Moscow are barely better equipped. Toilet paper is universally absent. ''Turkish toilets'' are not only widespread in the southern republics but can be found in Moscow as well. In many restaurants the dining tables are wiped with rags bearing close resemblance to floor rags. The entrances to some prestigious buildings in Moscow are adorned with larger rags which serve as floor mats, despite the fact that modern doormats seem widely available in Estonia.

Pollution levels are high in all the cities and industrial areas. As in most of Western Europe, cars are not equipped with antipollution devices. And since Soviet cars are not well maintained and the gasoline has less octane, the result is much more pollution per vehicle. Factories also lack modern antipollution devices. The once pristine waters of Lake Baikal are now polluted, many beautiful Karelian lakes are dead, and the air over Moscow is unhealthy. It is only very recently that the authorities, spurred to a large extent by a surge of public concern and by the Chernobyl accident, became conscious of the danger of pollution. While Soviet environmental problems are not unique, what made things worse was the dogmatic belief that such problems arise from a capitalist disregard of nature for profit's sake and cannot exist under Soviet conditions. This attitude prevented the country from taking adequate measures against something theoretically absent. Current efforts to cope with the problem are genuine and serious, but it will be hard to make up for lost time.

Crowding and noise are characteristic of slum conditions in any country, and especially in the poor areas of the Mediterranean countries. In the USSR the streets are not noisy by our standards: there are fewer cars and fewer stores, and order is better maintained. But restaurants take the pleasure of providing their customers with blaring music, rendering all conversation impossible. Recreational areas, on the other hand, are much quieter: there are not enough portable stereos to make life miserable, and order in public places is enforced. Urban transportation is very inexpensive and generally efficient. Subways, which have been built in most large cities in the USSR, are clean and quiet: music, grafitti, littering, and loitering are not tolerated. There are no homeless in the subways or railroad stations: if there were, they

Voices

"In our town [Ufa] there are queues not only for sausages but for every little thing: in the clinic, at the post office, at the savings bank, for public transportation. Almost all our spare time is spent in queues. Nobody counts that time, nobody calculates it. It is a special additional payment for purchases."

"What's going on in the stores in our Cheliabinsk is an outrage. The whole week you work under pouring rain out in the fields. On Saturday, you go to the store to buy the bare necessities, and you learn: That there is no washing powder, toothpaste, soap, butter, oil, margarine, or sausage—there is nothing! And if something appears, there's such a queue, you couldn't possibly get it."

From letters published in "The Queue,"
Izvestiia, October 24, 1987

would be removed immediately by the authorities and shipped away (to hospitals, jails, or state farms, as the case may be). Housing is crowded by our standards, but not very noisy: again, public order is usually enforced.

The worst problem is access to goods and services. There is a shortage of goods in stores, of seats in restaurants and theaters, of spare parts in service stations and repair outlets. There are long lines in front of anything desirable. It is a minor victory to obtain something, whether a roll of toilet paper or a seat for a good play. This situation forces people to spend hours searching, waiting, standing in lines, wasting their time. The number of hours per week devoted to shopping or getting something repaired is much greater than in any Western country, and the problem of wasted hours is now being openly debated in Soviet publications. With not enough after-work time left for all their essential errands, employees take time off from their jobs or stay on the phone in order to secure needed goods, decreasing the already low productivity of the Soviet workforce.

Green space is the best element of Soviet urban life. Not only have prerevolutionary parks been preserved, but new ones have been established in many areas. Often pompously called ''parks of culture and rest,'' they provide a pleasant oasis in the urban landscape.

The element most difficult to define, urban ''pleasantness,'' is far from abundant in Soviet city life. Small districts filled with cafes, bookstalls, specialty stores, and strolling passersby are very rare. Streets are lined with uniform facades, and the infrequently spaced shops exhibit dull storefronts. Large impersonal eating places are far apart. There is very little to catch the eye of the passerby. Exceptions to this rule are few: the recently created pedestrian mall in the Arbat in Moscow, the narrow streets of the old city of Tallin, a small walking area in old Tbilisi, and a few more. The success of the Arbat experiment in recreating a lively urban atmosphere brings some hope that more will be forthcoming. A few of the newly established cooperative restaurants have succeeded in overcoming the usual blandness of standard Soviet eating establishments. Until recently Moscow had only a dozen restaurants of quality, all state-owned.

Wandering on the streets of Moscow—outside of the few pleasant spots and far from the architectural wonders of prerevolutionary vintage—one feels a vacuum. There are wide impersonal avenues laid out in the 1930s. Buildings have an institutional appearance, with unwashed facades and dirty doorways. The six Stalin ''wedding cake'' skyscrapers, modern-day Roman hills, stand as lonely witnesses to the dictator's imperial dreams, while the new Hammer Center, restricted to foreigners, looks out of sync with its surroundings.

In Leningrad, a city fortunately untouched by the ''modernization drives'' of the 1930s, the beauty of the past contrasts sharply with the blandness of the present: instead of the elegant ladies of tsarist days stepping down from stylish carriages on to the famous Nevsky Prospect, one sees only long lines of tired customers waiting before decrepit storefronts.

The glamour of our Western cities, the skyscrapers of New York, the lights of Paris, the cafes of the Via Venetto, the shoppers at London's Harrods, the strollers in Greenwich Village or the Latin Quarter, are all absent from Soviet city life. Our vitality comes from private endeavors, multiplied a thousandfold. The grayness of the Soviet cityscape is the result of impersonal attempts to construct a public environment with little regard for individual human needs. The result is an urban atmosphere as "*gemütlich*" as a New York City housing project.

Viewed in their totality, Soviet cities are no great places to live. Some, like Leningrad, offer the splendor of the imperial past; others like Kiev, Vilnius, Tallin, and Lvov manage to combine the feeling of history with a cozier way of life. Moscow, being the union capital, attracts high achievers, whether in theater, academia, or science, but it is unable to match the vibrancy and vitality of Paris, Rome, London, or New York.

The Way of Life

21

The Workplace

The Soviet urban workplace can be divided into three basic categories:

- the factory (a production unit), with managerial, technical, clerical, and blue-collar staff;
- the service establishment, from restaurant to shoe repair shop, dealing directly with the customer;
- the office (*uchrezhdenie*), with managerial and clerical staff; a bureaucratic establishment, it has no direct contacts with customers in the sense of selling, serving, or repairing.

With some minor, and mostly recent, exceptions, all three categories are state-owned and -managed.

A Soviet enterprise is usually staffed in the following manner:

- the director, almost always a party member (and, in the case of a very large enterprise, a member of the *nomenklatura* as well);
- the party organizer (*partorg*), who represents the party in the enterprise (each enterprise has at least a party cell, larger ones a whole party organization), but most often has a lower party standing than the director himself. His main task is to support the director and help the factory fulfill its obligations; but, if the situation warrants, he can also report on the director's shortcomings;
- the union organizer, who is mostly involved in allocating vouchers to resort hotels, checking working conditions, arranging leaves of absence with pay for pregnant women, and the like.

He is not involved with issues of wages, working hours, or over-
time, all of which remain outside the union domain in the USSR;
   • the chief accountant, who is not only in charge of bookkeep-
ing but approves all expenses. He can be overruled by the director
at the latter's risk;
   • the deputy director (*zam*), one or several, who work under
the chief executive;
   • the head of the personnel department, whose task is to keep
track of employees' records and share the information with the
state security agency, the KGB. It is the personnel department
that bars some candidates from being hired on political grounds,
checks employees' autobiographies, and keeps their labor books
(into which merits, demerits, promotions, demotions, etc. are
inscribed);
   • department heads, section heads, security guards, maintenance personnel, clerical staff, and others make up the rest.
   Larger enterprises offer some amenities to their employees—a
cafeteria, sporadic distribution of better quality meats and gro-
ceries, hard-to-get tickets to shows, vouchers for vacation re-
sorts. Some can provide even more: help with police registration
(*propiska*) for new employees needing permission to reside in a
locale, access to better clothing, even some priority on a waiting
list for housing.

   A Soviet office, when compared with a Western one, seems
overstaffed, crowded, and inadequately equipped. There are innumerable clerks performing detail work, filling in vouchers by
hand, entering items into ledgers, and copying records, methods
characteristic of our turn-of-the-century office. The office equipment is old-fashioned. Electric typewriters, copying equipment,
computers, and so forth are extremely rare. One can still see an
abacus on the desk, sometimes alongside a modern calculator.
   The work tempo in a Soviet office is on the slow side. There are
lots of breaks, chats on the telephone with friends, long lunches.
There is plenty of time off for personal affairs and loitering in
corridors with fellow employees. All this is routine. Higher-ups

tend to behave more formally than is customary in the United States. This is not a peculiarly Soviet attitude but rather a European one, since social status has always played a larger role there.

In a Soviet factory several aspects are different. Qualified workers make more money than most engineers, except for those in command positions. Moreover, the number of engineers is higher than in the West and the number of highly qualified workers lower. Security personnel are relatively numerous. In general, the proportion of those engaged in direct production is lower than in the West, while that of other employees (from managers to guards) is higher.

Soviet workers are not known for trying harder than their office counterparts, the low level of material incentive and the rarity of dismissals being the primary reasons for this lack of enthusiasm.

Being employed in trade or service is considered best among average jobs and certainly, materially, the most advantageous. It offers direct access to scarce goods and services, without subjecting the employee to pressures under which his counterpart in a capitalist country is forced to perform. Thus, a Soviet waiter does not run, a salesclerk takes his time, a hotel maid takes it easy, repairmen do the customer a favor, and so on.

Work relations in trades and services are very much colored by the desirability of the position involved. In some republics of the southern belt, jobs in such fields cannot be obtained without substantial under-the-table payment to the hiring boss (in Azerbaijan, the minimum payment is said to be 1,000 rubles, and some very sought-after jobs are "sold" for tens of thousands). Smooth working relations are very important under these circumstances: when everyone around is involved in some illegalities—trading favors, accepting bribes, or simply stealing—internal conflicts that could lead to denunciations are very much feared. This is probably one of the reasons why organized trade and service fraud is more frequently found in Transcaucasia, Central

Voices

"You cannot just go out and locate the real black market. The good life cannot start on Monday: Contacts have to be established, the right connections have to be secured, the necessary useful friends and solid businesslike acquaintances have to be cultivated.

. . . Generally, black market activity brings undeniable results: for the country as a whole, spending by employees working in state trade is 60 percent higher than their official incomes; in one of the republics, trade and service employees own 70 percent of all the foreign cars (Renaults, Pontiacs, Mercedes, Volvos, etc.)."

From *Ogonek*, September 1987

Asia, and the Baltic republics, while in Russia proper simple theft or graft prevails. In Russia, social solidarity is lower, so jealousy of a neighbor's good luck is more acute and the propensity for denunciations historically higher.

The appearance of the Soviet storefront or of an enterprise's letterhead seems strange to a foreigner. We are used to a vivid display of brand names, corporate logos, or proprietors' names. The Soviet way is totally different. Brand names exist, but they are rare (except for cigarette brands). Most of the enterprises carry the names of leaders (the Lenin Factory, for example), or simply a number, such as Gastronom N. 3 (food market number 3). Along the streets one sees such signs as "Bakery," "Dairy Products," "Drinks," with no identifying proper name. This anonymity of distribution reinforces the indifference of the retail trade to the needs of the customer.

The key peculiarity of the Soviet workplace is its traditional independence from the profit motive: factories and stores operate like government offices. Quantitative fulfillment of the plan has been the main success criterion, ensuring bonuses and praise. Employees are therefore unconcerned about the quality of their products, their reception by customers, energy savings, the whole array of worries common to a capitalist enterprise.

Only after Gorbachev's coming to power did principles of cost accounting begin to penetrate the Soviet economy in a more consistent and serious way. One of the leading proponents of change, Academician Tatiana Zaslavskaia, listed six necessary reforms if Soviet enterprises are to be made responsive to the market forces from which they were intentionally severed. Translated from technical Russian into plain English, they are as follows:

- to reduce nepotism;
- to make merit, not something else [the party card?], the key to professional advancement;
- to support personal initiative;
- to relate employees' pay to genuine performance;
- to adjust prices to costs and abolish variations in the value of wages resulting from differential access to goods and services;
- to make families share the burden of taking care of those who cannot work, instead of leaving all such problems to the state.

As one can see, the main emphasis in this approach to reform is on freeing personal initiative from existing restrictions and compensating performance instead of seniority, connections, or loyalty. But it is not surprising that such proposals encounter a great deal of resistance. At this moment it is too early to judge whether the new Law on the State Enterprise and other reforms that Gorbachev introduces will succeed in altering the old mentality and instill new concerns into the minds of the employees of Soviet state enterprises.

22

Women's Roles

The situation of women in the USSR is paradoxical: despite the country's ideological and legal commitment to full equality, women clearly suffer a de facto lower status. To gain some understanding of this special situation, one has to reach back to pre-revolutionary times and then review the present-day peculiarities point by point.

In tsarist Russia women were legally discriminated against. The popular saying was that Russian women were so strong-minded that if they were given equal rights they would dominate their husbands (and many did anyhow). However, religious tradition, as reflected in the influence of such seventeenth-century writings as the *Domostroi* (House Regime), and Russia's history (no Renaissance or Age of Chivalry), are probably more realistic explanations.

Russian women were deprived of voting rights at all levels, from a voice in the peasant *mir* to a vote in the consultative assemblies of the early twentieth century. Divorces were next to impossible to obtain, and children of divorce "belonged" almost automatically to their fathers.

It was only at the turn of the present century that women began to filter into the professions: previously they had been confined to jobs such as governess, seamstress, maid, teacher, entertainer, or farmhand. Still, these factual restrictions seem to weigh less than historical tradition: Russia was not much different from other European countries as far as women's rights were concerned, but by and large it was more "oriental" in its attitudes toward women.

In most peasant households and in many conservative urban families, the old habit of corporal punishment of women and children never disappeared. Dowry was the rule, and in some Cossack areas the young girls went to country fairs wearing ribbons inscribed with the sum of the dowry offered. New brides lived with their husband's family and worked under the supervision of their mother-in-law.

In the Muslim south, the situation of women was much worse. Women wore veils, marriages were always prearranged, polygamy was accepted, and wives were bought from their fathers according to the custom of *kalym* (which still survives in many areas). In Russia, education for women, except for the upper classes, was very limited; in the Muslim areas it was almost nonexistent.

In legal terms the revolution changed almost everything and did so practically overnight. Women were given full equality with men. They were given voting rights, access to all the professions and trades, equal pay for equal work, and the right to divorce and to child support (but not alimony, which was seen as contradictory to the principle of equality). Eventually the same laws were introduced in the Muslim areas, but in view of local resistance, their implementation leaves something to be desired, even in our day.

As a result of all the changes brought about since the revolution, the Soviet woman plays an extremely important role in the economic life of the country. She accounts for roughly half of the Soviet labor force and the majority in many professions, including medicine, law, education, retail trade, and agriculture.

But despite the advancement of women, many of the realities of Soviet life undermine the whole concept of equality of the sexes.

• Equal pay for equal work is the rule, but women are far from occupying equal positions with men and consequently, on the average, receive lower salaries. Thus in medicine women prevail

Voices

"One of the most important principles of socialism is equal wages for equal work, and in our country this principle was realized a long time ago with regard to women. Men and women receive the same wages for the same work. Nonetheless, the average female wage is substantially lower than the average male wage. . . . If we compare the differentiation of male and female wages for our sample as a whole . . . we find the following: Whereas almost one-third of women earned less than one 100 rubles [per month], only 2 percent of men did so. Whereas the modal (typical) wage of women was 100–140 rubles, that of men was 180–240 rubles. The relative proportion of women with a wage above 250 rubles was negligible."

N. Rimashevskaia in *Sotsialisticheskii trud*, 1987, No. 7

among lower-paid general practitioners, while men predominate in surgery. In agriculture, women constitute the bulk of manual laborers, while men tend to be tractor drivers, brigadiers, and technicians. In trade, women stand behind the counter, while men dominate management and control. This is not much different from the situation in capitalist countries, but goes contrary to claims of de facto equality of sexes.

• There are no women in high governmental positions and, with only a few token exceptions, there have not been any since the revolution. The Soviet Union has failed to produce such women as Thatcher, Ghandi, Meir, or Weil. Among the revolutionaries, Nadezhda Krupskaia, after all, was known as Lenin's wife, Rosa Luxemburg lived in Germany, and Alexandra Kollontai never made it to the top. The age of Tsaritsas in St. Petersburg ended in the eighteenth century with the death of Catherine the Great, who in any case was German.

• Most women work alongside their husbands and also take

**Sharing of Household Duties
(1981, Russian Republic only)**

Shared	25%
Wife does two-thirds	16%
Wife does two-thirds to 90%	40%
Wife does alone	9%
Husband does alone	2%

Source: From a survey by the journal *Smena*, reported in V. I. Perevedentsev, *Sovetskaia molodezh' 80-kh godov* (Moscow, 1987).

care of their children, do the family shopping, cook the dinners, and keep the house clean. While this is also commonplace in the West, Soviet conditions of permanent shortages, endless queues, lack of many domestic appliances and other conveniences, and inadequate housing make the double burden much harder. Moreover, the wife's salary is even more indispensable in the Soviet Union than in the West.

• Difficult housing conditions, especially the need for young couples to wait a long time before getting housing, places an additional burden on the young wife. Living with parents, in communal apartments, or in dormitories, is not conducive to marital peace.

• Drunkenness among men, a frequent occurrence, increases marital difficulties. Among women, it is statistically less frequent: only a fifth of the alcoholics are women (still a large percentage by Western standards). Wife beating, child neglect, and squandering of household funds are direct consequences of this situation.

• Under the pretense of equality, women are often channeled into physically strenuous jobs in sanitation, construction, or heavy farm labor, a situation rare in the West. The image of an old woman cleaning the sidewalk with a small broom is not very inspiring.

• Despite undeniable achievements in the provision of basic

**Divorce
(1981, urban Russia only)**

Divorces initiated by the wife	73%
Causes:	
alcoholism	35%
infidelity	10%
jealousy	5%
housing conditions	7%
husband's unwillingness to share household duties	3%

Source: From a survey by the journal *Smena*, reported in V. I. Perevedentsev, *Sovetskaia molodezh' 80-kh godov* (Moscow, 1987).

health care, the services offered do not always meet women's needs. Thus in the European areas of the country women all too often resort to abortion for lack of reliable means of birth control. In the Muslim south, where birthrates are high, the high incidence of infant mortality reflects a lack of adequate postnatal care as well as poor sanitary conditions.

• In case of divorce (and the Soviet divorce rate is quite high outside of Muslim areas), women can count on child support, but not on alimony, unless they are invalids (the same, reciprocally, applies to men). A child is entitled to 25 percent of his father's salary, two children to 33 percent, and three to 50 percent, until the age of eighteen. But under Soviet conditions it is often not so much the salary but the fringe benefits that count (access, connections, privileges, priorities), and these cannot be so easily shared after divorce.

• The wives of men in power are supposed to stay in the background. The Soviet press shies away from exposing the private lives of prominent citizens. Gorbachev's attitude is rather exceptional: his wife travels with him abroad and is active within the country, something never seen under Brezhnev, Andropov, or Chernenko, and not necessarily approved. Khrushchev took his wife abroad, but that was the limit of her participation. Stalin's life was kept totally private, and only Krupskaia, Lenin's wife, played a role of her own.

• With clothing being very expensive, of poor quality, and difficult to obtain, Soviet women have a real problem in keeping up appearances. Outside the Baltic republics, where some good quality clothing is available, the struggle to dress well consumes a great deal of time and an even greater amount of money. This strains the family budget and leads to disputes with the husband, especially if the latter is neither well connected nor well paid. It introduces a heavy dose of ''petty bourgeois'' mentality into the life of the Soviet middle class.

• The usual shortage of fruits and vegetables (except in the southern belt) and a diet rich in starch and fats make it difficult for most Soviet women to stay slim, something of prime concern for the young generation.

There are, of course, regional differences in the conditions of women's lives. Thus in the Muslim areas women tend to be even less numerous in positions of importance, are much more dominated by family influences, and are less prone to divorce. Their husbands, however, tend to take on a greater share of the burden in raising the children, and alcoholism is much less common.

Only recently has the Soviet leadership begun to pay more attention to the shortcomings in women's status in the country. Attempts are now being made to promote women to more responsible positions, to avoid using women in hard labor, to enforce the collection of child support, and to provide some of the amenities of life that formerly were assigned low priority.

23

Youth

Every revolution glamourizes youth as the mainstay of the new regime. Propaganda posters from the early Soviet years show healthy young revolutionaries fighting elderly degenerate reactionaries. The latter were not only physically out of shape (capitalists with fat bellies and effete-looking aristocrats), but they looked outdated in their spats and monocles. Soldiers of the revolution, on the other hand, were not only vigorous and strong but also clad in line with the new revolutionary dress code.

Statues of young workers with hammers and peasants with sickles adorn many Soviet public places, offering a visible image of the new order. Soviet novels glamourizing revolution and civil war extol youthful heroes. The teenager Pavka Korchagin defends the revolution against decadent Polish noblemen. The young Pavlik Morozov denounces his "kulak" father. "We are the future, you are the past," they proclaim.

From the outset, special attention has been devoted to the needs of Soviet youth, the future of the new society. Except for children of deportees, many young people experienced none of the harsh realities of life in Stalin's time until they entered the labor market and had to earn a living for their families.

Schools, kindergartens, day-care centers, summer camps, and "Pioneer" palaces were given priority by the regime, to educate new cohorts devoted to the Cause. At the outset of the new era (in the early 1920s), children were given a voice in the running of schools, discipline was relaxed, and denunciations of parents were encouraged. In time all such extreme concessions were withdrawn; the last ones disappeared after Stalin's death.

By the time World War II ended, Soviet schools were well-organized and disciplined places, where properly dressed children followed a strict curriculum, all postrevolutionary "nonsense" having been forgotten long before. Still, children remained privileged in all other respects and as much as possible were sheltered from everyday hardships.

According to age groups, children are enrolled in three successive organizations: Octobrists for the preschool and beginning grades (ages five to nine), Pioneers, similar to our scouts, for ages ten to fifteen, and the Communist Youth League (Komsomol) for high schoolers and young adults. Octobrists parade with red scarves, Pioneers with red ties, Communist Youth with slogans (not their own, but those officially published prior to important holidays, such as May Day or November Seventh, the anniversary of the revolution). Groups, cells, and detachments are supposed to be constantly active with meetings, workshops, marches, sports events, lectures, singing, and a score of other activities. The idea is to keep the young busy, and well indoctrinated, with little time for outside temptations or an unchanneled social life. Between school and scheduled youth activities, there is not much time for anything else.

In general terms, and for a very long time, the regime was quite successful at keeping the allegiance of youth. It was less so in those republics where the family is very strong (such as among the Muslims), or religion survives (among Muslims and Catholics), or solidarity between the generations prevails (among the Baltic peoples as well as the above communities). But in the country at large, and regardless of the shocks to which adult society was repeatedly subjected during the harsh years of Stalin's reign, Soviet youth remained the most reliable sector of society, the regime's most fervent supporter, often blind to its faults, while trusting its aims, and always devoted to its leader.

This ideal situation began to deteriorate after World War II. To begin with, the young cohorts who as a group entered the war

Musical Tastes of Students (in % of respondents)

Preferred types of music	Boys	Girls
Symphonic	16	24
Soviet pop	8	65
Foreign pop	32	69
Soviet rock	58	24
Foreign rock	58	3
Jazz	8	1
Folk music	0	3
Ballads	12	10

Source: Derived from S. L. Kataev, ''The Musical Tastes of Youth,'' *Sotsiologicheskie issledovaniia*, 1986, no. 1.

grew up much faster than their elders, and often lost their illusions too fast for a safe landing. Then came Khrushchev's 1956 speech which toppled the image of Joseph Stalin as a father figure, and accelerated the decline of youth's trust in the leadership in general. Moreover, the regime's means of persuasion were no longer those of Stalin, and young people never fell prey to the fears prevalent in their fathers' generation. At the same time Western influence began to spread. In the era of transistors and cassette recorders it was difficult to maintain the isolation of the past. And finally, probably the most important factor, the Soviet leadership of the Brezhnev era became the epitome of the old guard. Moscow's leaders looked like solid members of a conservative board of directors, an image previously associated with ''old regimes.''

How can we possibly imagine an elderly member of Brezhnev's Politburo, with his outmoded suit, lumbering gait, and cautious demeanor, serving as a model for a jeans-clad young man of the 1970s, a rock music fan, an avid participant in the electronic age? For him, the failings of Nicholas II were ancient history, and so was Stalin. Moreover, the current leadership was clearly at death's door.

Voices

"I'm a Spartak fanatic. . . . My leader's favorite saying is: 'How boring life is, gentlemen, how boring.'
. . . Most of us aren't interested in sports. 'Fanaticism' is a way to self-affirmation and to set oneself apart. Some are distinguished by what they wear, some by music. . . .
One night I had no idea how to occupy myself. I went to the movies. Some film! Am I crazy to go to a movie like that? Then I ran into some kids. They offered me tickets to a disco in a club. . . . I met some companions. These kids invited me to a cafe and said they were 'fanatics.' I liked it. And I became one of them."

The words of Lena, an 18-year-old girl, in
Sotsiologicheskie issledovaniia, 1987, No. 1

This was precisely the situation when Gorbachev made his ascent to power. The official youth movement, well organized and state supported, but only very recently open to change, must contend with Soviet youth grown indifferent to the old organization, weary of long speeches, and uninterested in over-aged "youth leaders." Its new "groups" are spontaneous creations. Their leaders are natural leaders, not appointed by adults, their membership is fluid, and their purposes change with the fads or interests of the moment. Some groups identify themselves as "hippies," "punks," or sports "fanatics." Others are short-lived informal groups, brought together to facilitate social life and combat boredom and loneliness. Although official youth organizations manage to maintain their memberships (since repudiation is politically inadvisable), enthusiasm is lukewarm and many Komsomol members belong simultaneously to an informal group.

The aging of a revolutionary regime is not a phenomenon

Unofficial Youth Groups

Fanatics: Their goal is emotional discharge, to set oneself apart, and to demonstrate one's belonging through stylized outfits. . . . Being fans of a soccer club is only a pretext for common action.

Rockers: Their appearance, with minor modifications, is in the Western "punk" style. Ecstatic conduct at concerts and discos.

Breakers: Fans of break dancing. The First All-Union Break Festival ("Parrot '86") took place in Jurmala in 1986, the second in Kaunas ("Breakass '87").

Hippies: Split into three major groups. The "Old Generation" typically are fans of mysticism, Buddhism, and yoga, and use narcotics. The "Men of the System" have as declared goals self-expression and moral liberation, and have an interest in religious movements and mysticism. The "Pacifists" reject violence and regard any political system as a system of oppression.

Karate and kung-fu groups: A declared goal of physical and moral self-perfection, mastery of self-defense techniques, and other Eastern conceptions built around self-effacement and subordination to a guru.

Poppers: Their main objective is to pay no attention to the negative side of life and to take pleasure in what is. They display the hallmarks of "elitism"—fancy clothing and hairdos, elegantly correct speech.

Optimists: Their goal is to examine internal and external problems of the country's political development. "Optimists" use no alcohol or narcotics.

Environmental defense groups: "ECO," "Greens," "Flora," etc. Declared goal—defense of the environment, restoration of lost natural wealth.

Source: Derived from I. Iu. Sundiev, "Informal Youth Organizations," *Sotsiologicheskie issledovaniia,* 1987, No. 5.

unique to the USSR. It has happened many times before. But the victorious ring of finality in the October revolution was one of the strongest, the regimentation of its youth among the most efficient, and therefore its downtrend is all the more apparent. The aging of a regime is also accompanied by the aging of its values. They gradually lose their ability to transfix as they become conventions—something young people never admire. Then values no longer fulfill their initial promise, and a slow process of gradual devaluation sets in. Finally, "values" turn into slogans, the latter as dry and bureaucratic as the party apparatus itself. Youth is enthusiastic about change, challenge, and novelty, not about established norms, routine, and conformity. Official youth organizations still offer opportunities for meeting people and filling free time, but even this is often handled in too bureaucratic a manner compared with the cozier ambience of an informal group.

According to surveys conducted by Soviet sociologists, many young people who are "alienated from the formalities in Communist Youth activities" switch to informal groups. The newspaper *Komsomol'skaia pravda* estimates that approximately one-third of all Moscow high-school students belong to "gangs" with such names as "Metallists," "Breakers," "Rockers," "Kents" (after the American cigarette brand), "Serki" (from the Russian expression meaning bleak, gray, bored), "Nostalgists," and others. While most of the groups show signs of English or American inspiration, some turn to Russian sources, as if following the old split between liberal "Westernizers" and conservative "Slavophiles." Thus a gang in one suburb of Moscow not only are admirers of Arnold Schwarzenegger but proclaim Russian chauvinism as well. And we hear of another small group, by the name of "Ross," that follows the line of the adult group "Pamiat," a Russian chauvinist organization tolerated by the authorities.

Another survey complains that the use of religious symbols (crosses, icons, etc.) has doubled among young people during the last five years and that 40 percent of the young do go to church,

24

Fashion

The history of Soviet fashion awaits its author. The prerevolutionary style prevailing in the European urban centers of the old Romanov empire was patterned upon universally accepted European standards. Peasant dress, on the other hand, was still influenced by local tradition and varied from region to region. European influence began with Peter the Great, who forced the high nobility to shed its traditional ''oriental'' attire in favor of Western dress and manners. Initially limited to the aristocracy, Western ways spread during the eighteenth century to the lesser nobility, and during the nineteenth century to the bulk of city dwellers.

The October revolution put up a new wall between Western fashions and the new Soviet style. With Russia's higher classes dispossessed and dishonored, class distinctions in clothing narrowed tremendously. Shortages of high-quality apparel further reduced those distinctions. The ideal was to look like everybody else (*byt' kak vse*). All formal clothing vanished: tuxedos, evening gowns, formal headwear. Apparel associated with ''bourgeois'' taste followed suit. Men's hats gave way to caps, ladies' hats to scarves; high heels and ties were a rarity. Cosmetics were frowned upon. Fur coats became suspect.

At the same time, new ''revolutionary'' fashions began to emerge. At first they were modeled on soldiers' and sailors' outfits. Then, after Stalin's rise to power, came a vogue for his paramilitary style of dress: cap, tunic over the pants, boots. Every collective farm chairman dressed that way, and only a few stubborn eccentrics dared to be more formal. Among Soviet leaders, only Molotov dressed in a traditional men's suit.

Here one should note that Stalin's costume is in keeping with similar attire worn by other authoritarian leaders—Mussolini, Hitler, Mao, Castro, Qaddafi. Each has favored a characteristic outfit, recognizable by the masses as a symbol of the new order, and inevitably, the leader's appearance exerted a strong influence on the country's fashions.

Stalin's death brought about the demise of his costume just as Mao's death would end the monopoly of his favorite jacket in the People's Republic of China. ''Bourgeois'' clothing reappeared, as did cosmetics. By the time Brezhnev came to power, all Politburo members wore regular suits, hats, and ties.

With political relaxation, young people are the first to catch new trends: sport clothing, narrow pants, jeans, zippered jackets, sweatshirts with foreign emblems or inscriptions. The middle class, still getting accustomed to three-piece suits, is gradually embracing the gamut of modern fashion. With the satisfaction of basic clothing needs, except among the poorest, style and quality have acquired much greater importance. Imports, especially from the right countries, are highly regarded, while domestic products are looked down upon. Fake foreign labels, always printed in Latin characters, appear on local goods, while Cyrillic letters convey an outdated image.

Class differences in clothing are becoming more obvious. ''Better people'' wear clothing imported from the West, those lower on the social ladder dress in East European clothes, and the masses have to be content with either domestic or third world goods of inferior quality and style. Some trendy Muscovites pride themselves on wearing only imported Western clothing and spend a good deal of money and energy to achieve the desired result.

Regional differentiation is also of importance. Thus, in highly Westernized Estonia, local brands are of good quality, even in ready-to-wear. Moscow offers some choice, but only to those with the right connections or cash, little to the general public. American products are the most desirable; French goods are prized by the more sophisticated public.

Citizens from provincial towns around Moscow shop in the capital. Visitors from the southern republics, from Transcaucasia to Central Asia, also shop in Moscow and are willing to pay way above the official price for imported goods.

One fashion of the revolutionary era that survives to this day is leather. Initially the distinctive outfit of Red Army commissars during the civil war, leather outerwear remained popular, although there have been some alterations in style. Thus not only military-style jackets but all kinds of leather coats are in fashion. Leather pants and stylish ladies' boots carry an exorbitant price on the black market and seem to be the dream of the younger set. Leather is so desirable that in New York it is possible to recognize a recent Soviet immigrant by his leather outerwear, bought in Italy on the way to the States.

Jewelry evolved the way the clothing did. After having all but disappeared after the revolution, it gradually came back to levels comparable (in quantity if not in quality) to the rest of Europe. Even the wearing of religious symbols, such as crosses, has become popular and is not necessarily any indication of the religious beliefs of the wearer.

In the field of high fashion, the USSR is still far behind the rest of Europe. Fashion shows are a very recent phenomenon and have been mostly staged by Western designers. Prices for dressmaking are in the vicinity of 25 rubles, and tailoring a men's suit costs more than twice that amount (material excluded). Ready-to-wear dresses cost 50–70 rubles and men's suits 150–200 rubles. Made-to-order footwear seems limited to simple items exhibited at the shop and not worthy of special expense.

Regional differences are, as always, important: the Baltic republics fare the best, followed by Moscow and the richer southern republics such as Georgia or Armenia. Russian and Muslim provincial areas are at the bottom rungs of the fashion ladder.

In furniture, Soviet tastes recall the 1950s, when the so-called Scandinavian modern styles conquered the market. Walls with components and a lot of glass, area rugs (wall-to-wall carpets never made it to the USSR), wallpaper, modern chairs and tables are common in Soviet households. Hotel beds are unusually narrow. At home, twin beds predominate and double beds are not very common; queen or king sizes are unheard of. Middle-class households have basic modern appliances but no luxuries such as dishwashers.

Again, regional differences play their role: more rugs and upholstery in the south, more glass in the north, better quality woods in the Baltic region.

The evolution of manners *grosso modo* follows that of fashion. Certainly, it is difficult to speak of "Soviet" manners, given the enormous range of cultures that exist in the USSR.

The prerevolutionary manners of the upper classes, those normally imitated (whether successfully or not) by the rest of the population, were speedily discarded after the revolution. Taking one's hat off when entering a house was no longer the thing to do, since this old custom was seen as akin to uncovering one's head in church. Hand kissing, an old Eastern European tradition, was sacrificed on the altar of equality between the sexes. Standing up when a lady or an older person entered the room, courtesy at the door, civility on public transportation and in the streets—all went overboard. The manners that surfaced in the Russian cities after the revolution were at best those of revolutionary sailors.

It was possibly Stalin's conservative tastes that restored some old-fashioned politeness in common behavior by the 1940s. Thus with the return to the old military insignia in the armed forces came a more genteel reevaluation of manners as well. Students at the prestigious Moscow Institute of Foreign Relations received lessons in dance and etiquette, including the proper way to handle forks and knives. This acceptance of proper behavior among the most privileged spread downward to the upper echelons of the middle class as well. Still, during Stalin's time, the average Soviet party boss or industrial manager tended to be ill-mannered by any standard.

During the post-Stalin years, the return to better manners

accelerated. Today, Soviet citizens behave no worse than their
Western counterparts, and sometimes better. Older people do
have a chance to get a seat on the bus, and only low-class people
enter a room with their hats on. If etiquette suffers now, this is
attributable to the imitation, rather than rejection, of Western
norms as seen in imported Western movies and in tourist behavior.

It is particularly in the realm of etiquette that regional differences remain profound. In the Muslim areas, hospitality is as
always very strong, although women are rarely given priority at
the door or in seating. In the Baltic republics, manners follow
closely those prevailing in Eastern and Central Europe. In Russia
proper, social differences govern manners: the higher classes
have largely returned to the civilized ways of their prerevolutionary predecessors, modified here and there, while the lower
classes show a mixture of traditional politeness and postrevolutionary rudeness, resulting in a kind of Soviet "muzhik" behavior.

Manners and fashion reflect tastes as well. In the Western
borderlands, in the Baltic states, and among better-off Muscovites and capital dwellers in the other republics, tastes are more
sophisticated. In the rest of the country, popular taste predominates. Here again, the younger set takes the lead, even in provincial towns. Young Russian women try to stay slim instead of
following their mothers' example. Muslim young men no longer
see a big paunch as a sign of opulence. Sharply dressed young
people can be seen in many places, a sure sign of the abandonment of revolutionary garb, manners, and taste.

Still, there is always some time gap between the USSR and the
West. Thus the preference for natural products, whether in dress
(natural cotton and pure wool as opposed to synthetics) or food
(no additives or chemicals) has not yet reached the USSR, except
for those highest on the social ladder, or urbanites in the Baltic
republics.

The Soviet Union remains highly diversified in fashion, manners, and taste. A young upper-class Muscovite lady looks as fashionable as her Western European counterpart. An Azeri woman, in her native village, looks and behaves like her counterpart in Turkish Anatolia. A middle-aged Estonian lady, properly dressed, emerges from a Viennese-style cafe. A sturdy Russian matron looks the way we imagine she should look. But the war between European-inspired style and "proletarian" taste has ended, with the victory of the first and the persistence of the latter only in remote corners of the country and among society's losers.

Of all the usual components of a family budget—shelter, food, clothing, entertainment, health, education, and so forth—nowhere is clothing as important as in the Soviet Union. And at least in this domain, de Gaulle's conception of Europe extending from the Atlantic to the Urals has been proven right. In fashion, manners, and taste, the country has made its choice loud and clear.

25

Sports

It seems that every one-party system cherishes and supports sports—witness Nazi Germany and fascist Italy as well as the Soviet Union in the Stalin era. Victory in sports is seen as proof of the superiority of the nation or system that presumably made these achievements possible. For Hitler, excellence in sports proved the superiority of the German race, for Stalin—the superiority of the socialist system. Given the important propaganda value attached to athletic performance, the government does its utmost to lend its support and to honor national sports heroes. Today, however, there is less emphasis on sports as an opportunity to prove superiority and more on their value in supporting friendly international relations.

The Soviet sports scene exhibits several peculiarities:
• the great popularity of soccer, gymnastics, and chess (considered a sport in the Soviet Union), and the absence of American-style football or baseball;
• little emphasis on college sports as a mass event, very much in contrast with the mass appeal of college sports in the United States;
• an absence of "rich man's sports," such as polo, golf, and car racing, although there are some racetracks;
• a pretense of "amateurism," maintained in all sports at least until very recently;
• obviously, no privately owned clubs, teams, and the like, and no tradition of endorsement of sporting goods by athletes (al-

though recently some Soviet athletes have endorsed foreign goods while taking part in international competitions);

• the "defection" of a Soviet athlete on tour abroad is still seen as a betrayal—and as evidence of a lack of vigilance by coaches, team-mates, and supervisors. Soviet athletes have not been allowed to play on foreign teams, but rumors abound about a possible relaxation of this rule, especially for hockey players.

Originally, the Soviet regime favored only team sports and frowned upon individual ones, the group effort carrying a communal connotation as opposed to the glorification of individual, and therefore egotistic effort. Soccer was supported, tennis disregarded. Only chess, so strongly ingrained in Russian tradition, did not suffer because of its individual nature. With time, the exclusive emphasis on group sports gave way to an acceptance of all sports, except for those that demanded too much outlay per individual athlete. Downhill skiing was less encouraged than cross-country. Gymnastics was favored: it requires only little equipment and space. Even today, the USSR is not a land of golf courses.

Until very recently, all Soviet sport was considered amateur, not professional. This created a strange situation. In many international competitions, Soviet athletes entered as "amateurs" met genuine foreign amateurs and won even in sports in which the Soviet Union is not particularly strong. This took place, for example, in Olympic boxing matches, from which the best American boxers were excluded as professionals. The Soviet athlete "employed" by a factory or office generally has a no-show job, and devotes 90 percent of his work time to practice and play. In this way, perhaps, the Soviet "amateur" athlete is not unlike some U.S. college "student" football or basketball stars.

The best Soviet athletes are privileged people. They not only get money, bonuses, and desirable apartments; they travel abroad, obtain cars, and receive a great deal of respect from their fellow citizens.

Soccer is the most popular sport, attracting the largest crowds, and commanding the greatest loyalty of its fans. Names of soccer teams are of "proletarian" inspiration. "Dynamo" and "Spartak" (for Spartacus, leader of a slave revolt in ancient Rome) are team names used across the country. Local patriotic feelings are on display during encounters, particularly if teams of different republics or countries are involved. Police are massively deployed during important games, and a few bloody riots have occurred in Soviet sports history, the best known being one that took place in Tashkent in the 1960s during an encounter between a local club and a Russian team.

Soviet sports facilities, stadiums, clubs, and training facilities are numerous and well kept. Sports news is widely followed, both in the press and on television. Fans are ardent and regional patriotism strong. Physical education for the young is widespread and excellent. There is no doubt that, except for the shaky pretense of the "amateurism" of the top sports teams and athletes, Soviet sports training is among the positive achievements of the regime.

Soviet participation at the summer and winter Olympics is an important event for the country, winning massive government support as well as a great deal of public attention. Amassing more Olympic medals than the United States is a point of honor, a kind of political victory.

The 1980 Moscow Olympics (boycotted by the United States because of the Soviet invasion of Afghanistan) was conducted as an event of considerable political importance. Not only were new sports facilities and modern hotels built, but thousands of undesirables, ranging from derelicts to dissidents, were expelled from Moscow for the duration of the games, the idea being to make the best possible impression on foreign visitors.

The future of Soviet sport looks bright. It is popular, financially well supported, with good training facilities, large numbers of eager participants, and mass audiences. Its athletes will profit if the current relaxation permits them to enter more worldwide events and gain more recognition abroad.

26

Alcohol and Narcotics

"The pleasure of Russia is drinking" goes an ancient Russian adage attributed to Prince Vladimir, who introduced Christianity to his country 1,000 years ago. It is from Vladimir's Kievan Rus that the three Eastern Slavic nations of Belorussia, Russia, and Ukraine have sprung. They all share the prince's taste for spirits (for vodka since the 1500s, when it first appeared in neighboring Poland). When Vladimir weighed the merits of Islam, the Koran's prohibition of drinking was seen as a serious flaw.

During the reign of Ivan the Terrible heavy drinking was an acceptable social occurrence. The income from the state alcohol monopoly was essential to the tsar's treasury, just as the tax on alcohol remains a major source of revenue in today's USSR.

When Alexei Mikhailovich was tsar (the seventeenth century), refusal to drink on official occasions was a punishable offense. The Dutch traveler Olivarius, who visited Moscow twice during that era, devoted many pages to drunkenness in Russia, replete with sexual and scatological details. Tsar Peter the Great so loved to drink that he established a "drunken court" with special ceremonies devoted to Bacchus.

The Russian drinking tradition is so old, so widespread, so ingrained, that it is almost impossible to visualize a Russian evening without vodka, a Russian wedding without drunkenness, or even a Russian novel without drinking episodes. But the distinguishing feature of the Russian way of drinking is not the per capita alcohol consumption (at the end of the nineteenth century Russia occupied only the twelfth place in the world) but the style

Voices

"We encounter real contradictions: alcohol undermines the economic, social, and moral fabric of the society; and whenever a social system stagnates, alcohol helps to keep it the way it is."

Sotsiologicheskie issledovaniia, 1987, No. 1

of drinking. The French or the Italians may drink more but they spread out their drinking through the week, and they drink mostly at meals. The Russian peasant, on the other hand, could drink only occasionally. But when he drank, he did it to the point of sliding "under the table." A Russian, traditionally, does not drink for pleasure or to accompany meals but to get drunk and forget the realities of everyday life.

Some interesting statistical data are provided by Dr. Boris Segal. According to Segal, in Russia of 1913, among those fifteen and older, the percentage of chronic alcoholics was estimated at 2 percent as opposed to 17 percent in 1985. During that period the per capita consumption of alcohol moved up from 3.7 liters to 29.5 liters (eightfold). Median expenditures for alcoholic beverages in an average family budget jumped from 1.3 percent in 1913 to 21.2 percent in 1985 (Soviet sources quote 16.2 percent, not a drastic difference). The incidence of alcohol-related illnesses increased nearly eightfold, from 3,784 per 100,000 to 31,182. Alcohol-related losses (in terms of missed work, poor workmanship, medical care, etc.) were estimated at 200 billion rubles per year in 1970, at half a trillion in the mid-1980s—a sum larger than the entire all-union budget. According to Segal, alcoholism accounts for a 30 percent downturn in productivity on Mondays, for 70 percent of manslaughters, and 90 percent of hooliganism. Even allowing for possible errors, recent

Voices

"It seemed that more pressure, interdiction, limitations, and a price increase for vodka [would work], so . . . ?

It was increased. And forbidden. And limited. But general sobriety failed to materialize. In the wake of futile prohibitive measures, came a murky wave of home brews, cologne, toothpaste, shoe polish, chloroform . . . narcotics addiction and abuse of toxic substances. And their sure consequence—poisoning."

"Because of the dry law, simple working people have no more holidays. Everyone walks around mad as a jackal."

From letters quoted in *Izvestiia*, October 3, 1987

Soviet data edge close to his figures, especially in evaluating the part of alcohol in the average family budget. However, given the poor reporting of social data prior to World War I, Segal's 1913 figures seem low: the incidence of alcoholism in prerevolutionary Russia was probably closer to current figures. The disturbing fact, however, is that 18 percent of alcoholics in the country today are said to be women. This was certainly not the case before the revolution.

Three attempts to force down the consumption of alcohol preceded Gorbachev's campaign, but they were all unsuccessful. The first such attempt occurred during World War I in the years 1914–16, the second between 1919 and 1925, and the third in 1972. Each time, alcohol emerged victorious. The last attempt (1972) was aimed at making Russians drink less vodka and other hard liquors and switch to wine and beer. But the aim was defeated by "strengthening" the wine and by the Russian habit of drinking until drunk, regardless of what is consumed.

The most recent campaign, initiated in May 1985, was aimed

Voices

"In the village everybody makes homebrew, every household."
"And you too, granny? Why?"
"What do you mean, why? We are war widows. Who is going to
fix the roof, deliver the coal, repair the fence, bring in the potatoes?
Money, they don't take. Liquor store spirits are out of reach now.
And I need to get workmen. Yesterday the vet's helper spayed the
hog. He used to settle for three rubles, now he wants a bottle."

From a conversation reported in "Potholes in the
Road to Sobriety," *Pravda*, October 19, 1987

at reducing all alcohol consumption, be it wine, beer, or hard
liquor. The measures initially consisted of limiting the number of
retail outlets and opening hours, reducing the number of restaurants with liquor licenses, forbidding restaurants to serve alcoholic beverages before 2 p.m., curtailing production itself,
switching some wine distilleries to juice production, and finally
uprooting some vineyards altogether. The overall results, however, have been far from satisfactory.

Enforcement of some anti-alcohol measures borders on the
impossible. The uprooting of established vineyards in the southern republics was economically unwise, and the local population
knew it. In the north, vodka queues grew nasty; long lines of grim
customers would push and grumble. On one reported occasion,
overzealous local authorities posted policemen at nine wedding
parties to enforce a local nondrinking ordinance. (The ordinance
was issued following a drunken-driving accident that occurred
after a previous wedding party.)

A bottle of vodka often replaces legal currency as the common
payment unit: even prior to the "dry law" many Russians used to

count their income in the numbers of vodka bottles that salary could buy.

True, during 1986 the Soviet per capita consumption of officially sold alcoholic beverages dropped by half. But the figure is misleading. During the same year, the consumption of sugar, a basic ingredient for distilling alcohol, rose by a billion kilos (2.2 billion pounds), enough to distill 10 billion bottles of *samogon* (home-brewed vodka). That translates into an additional three bottles per month for every man, woman, and child in the land, bringing the per capita consumption back to the old figure. Rationing of sugar was imposed to arrest that trend.

Thus, the "dry law" opened a Pandora's box of new problems, all related to the difficulty of getting this highly desirable "liquid" commodity. The reopening of many wine and beer bars in 1988 and the decision to allow larger beer production were the first concessions, and by the end of that year the anti-alcohol campaign seemed to have folded.

The usage of narcotics in the Soviet Union was denied for a long time: it was supposedly a purely capitalist addiction, something connected with the "decay of capitalist society" and absent from Soviet life. Lately, however, the spread of drug addiction in the USSR has been acknowledged, and Soviet television has even shown police raids on illegal poppy fields. It has been said that many Soviet young men got their first exposure to narcotics during military service in Afghanistan. Still, we should keep in mind that the Soviet drug problem is only a fraction of ours and that in the USSR alcoholism, not drugs, is the main social scourge.

There are other ways in which Soviet drug problems differ from ours. Among addicts, the proportion of young people seems much higher in the Soviet Union, probably because drug addiction is a more recent phenomenon. It seems to be equally spread among all nationalities and not higher among minorities. Another difference is that whereas in the United States the bulk of narcotics is "imported," in the Soviet Union it is domestically pro-

Voices

"I smoke hashish and drink opium extract whenever and wherever. Someimes I pop pills too. I understand clearly how harmful this is. I want to quit but I don't have the strength. No way would I go to a hospital. They'd start an investigation, the police would get involved, there'd be a trial: Where did you get it? How did you get it?"

A letter quoted in *Literaturnaia gazeta*, August 20, 1986

duced, mostly in Central Asia but also in Russia itself, wherever hemp and poppies are grown (poppy seeds are a favorite ingredient in baked goods). On a few occasions Soviet territory has been used for transshipment of narcotics from the Middle East. The final destination, however, has been some hard-currency country, not the USSR.

The connection between drugs and crime is known, but in the Soviet Union the rate of drug-connected crimes is still much lower than the rate of alcohol-related crimes. Drug traffic exists, from medical institutions in Moscow to poppy fields near Kuibyshev, but the scale of organized drug traffic is much smaller than in our country. Still, arrests are growing, and in 1986 Moscow police arrested five times more youthful offenders than in the previous year (but the new number was only 776).

Uniformity and Diversity

27

Symbols and Slogans

Every state, regime, political party, public organization, and sports team, and almost every association, commercial society, and industrial establishment, has its own symbol or logo. This allows partisans, customers, and fans to recognize the bearer easily and to develop an allegiance to the program, club, or product symbolized. Even similar symbols may vary widely in their meanings. The Mercedes star, the Star of David, the Red Star, and the Stars and Stripes evoke different frames of reference and stir different reactions, depending on personal attitudes toward the set of values represented by each of these universally understood symbols. Similarly, we can easily distinguish the clenched fist, the stretched hand of the "hail" salute, the "V" sign, or the one-finger offensive gesture. (In seventeenth-century Russia a great deal of blood was shed when the old way of crossing oneself with two fingers was replaced by the new three-finger pattern.)

In many third world countries where illiteracy is widespread, voting is conducted with party logos, not written names. It is understood that any citizen should be able to recognize a party symbol quite easily. Whether it is an alligator on a polo shirt, an eagle on a car hood, an elephant or a donkey on a political poster, an effective symbol evokes a very specific image.

A revolutionary government, more than any other, is disposed to create its own world of symbols. Through immediate and easy recognition, it supplies a visual focal point for partisan allegiance and reinforcement of a major political theme. Thus, we can easily distinguish Mao's jacket or his "little red book" (even though we are unable to read it), or Castro's famous beard and his fatigues (tailor-made by now), not to mention his *"Cuba si! Yanqui no!"* slogan. Fascist regimes of the 1930s and early 1940s were no less involved with political sign language. Mussolini adopted symbols from ancient Rome. Hitler's *Hakenkreuz* and the SS emblem are familiar sights in B-rated World War II movies, and sometimes are painted by our home-grown hoodlums on the doors of Jewish synagogues.

The Soviet regime was from its very outset enamored of symbols and slogans. The illiteracy of the masses made these tools essential for effective allegiance-gathering.

Early revolutionary symbolism was directly connected with the theme of worker–peasant alliance and proletarian dictatorship. The hammer and sickle, an apt symbol of worker–peasant partnership, was adopted in 1918 to replace the imperial double eagle. The red banner, the international symbol of the workers' movement, unfurled by the revolutionaries in Paris in 1792 and since then by each consecutive proletarian movement, became the flag of the country, displacing the old tricolor. The red star, the symbol of unity among the workers of the five continents (sharing the same symbolic meaning as the clenched fist), appeared on flagposts, on the caps of the Red Guards, and over the Kremlin towers. The "International," the song of the international workers' movement since the time of the Paris Commune, became the national anthem in place of the English-inspired "God Save the Tsar."

People were to be addressed as comrades or citizens (as in the French revolution). At the beginning of the new regime these terms of address carried the connotation of solidarity, friendship, and equality, but such meaning was worn down with time. The word "citizen" in Russian has both masculine and feminine forms, while the word "comrade" (*tovarishch*) has no gender. Today, in the Soviet Union, "comrade" sounds like a kind of unisex Mr./Mrs./Ms., and "citizen" seems an appropriate designation for the recipient of a traffic summons or child support subpoena. Sometimes, in addressing an older woman, the word "madame" is used instead of the slightly embarrassing "comrade," but only foreigners may be addressed as *gospodin* (for a gentleman) or *gospozha* (for a lady).

After the revolution, a new vocabulary invaded the Russian language. Words like "the people" (*narod*), "the Party" (meaning only the Communist party), "the leader" (*vozhd'*), and "the struggle" were followed by an array of novel expressions: "*subbotnik*" (voluntary workday), "agitation and propaganda," "vanguard," "warmonger," "stooge," "parasite," "enemy of the people," etc. Hundreds of adjectives followed suit as the language itself became imbued with revolutionary symbolism. In addition, the language began to absorb two elements: the names, abbreviations, and acronyms of innumerable Soviet institutions, and the bureaucratic lingo born of the journalistic effort to conform the written word to the changing political winds (to the extent of lifting entire sentence structures from official pronunciamentos). These forms were then translated into the languages of other nationalities across the country.

Similarly, every component republic of the Soviet Union was given a flag and a shield of its own. The shields were not drastically different from one another, and the flags were limited to three colors, with red predominant. Each shield has to carry the words "Proletarians of the world, unite" in the language of the republic and in Russian. It is interesting that the shield of the Belorussian republic originally had that inscription in four languages—Belorussian, Russian, Polish and Yiddish. Since World War II, however, the last two have vanished from the shield, eradicating this unusual variation in Soviet heraldics.

When Stalin discarded the "International" as the country's anthem and replaced it with the newly written "Hymn of the Soviet Union," all the national republics were, in turn, supplied with their own national anthems modeled on the hymn, praising Russia, Lenin, Communism, and the Party, as well as their own

Anthem of the Latvian Soviet Socialist Republic

This precious land is where we got our freedom,
Where generation after generation is to be born happy,
Where the sea roars and the fields flourish,
And our towns bustle, Riga above all!
  Soviet Latvia shall live forever,
  And shine brightly among the Soviet nations!

We rose up to break the chains of slavery,
Every site here testifies to a centuries-long struggle,
Only together with the people of the great Russian land
Did we become a power that defeats the foe.
  Soviet Latvia shall live forever,
  And shine brightly among the Soviet nations!

We shall go Lenin's way toward happiness and glory,
With the flag of the October revolution, always.
We shall guard our Soviet fatherland
To our very last drop of blood, everyone.
  Soviet Latvia shall live forever,
  And shine brightly among the Soviet nations!
  Soviet Latvia shall live forever,
  And shine brightly among the Soviet nations!

land. Georgia remained an exception: her anthem fails to mention Russia by name, a concession granted his homeland by Stalin.

The Soviet republics' symbols have been much less successful than federal ones because they lack an essential element, namely, the necessary local flavor, tradition, or appeal. The shields contain minimal local imagery (for Azerbaijan, an oil rig). The anthems contain some reference to local geography, but not to history. The flags fail to represent anything traditional, except for some factual elements (for example, sea waves for Latvia). Thus, the lion of Georgia is absent from the Georgian flag, and the national colors of the Baltic republics bear no resemblance to those used prior to their annexation to the USSR. Similarly, the flags, shields, and anthems of the six predominantly Muslim republics lack Islamic symbols: no green, no crescent, no reference to the historic past. Perhaps as a consequence, very few citizens of a Soviet republic would even recognize their "own" flag, anthem, or shield. Recently the three Baltic republics restored the use of their pre-Soviet flags.

In Russia itself, at the time of the revolution, old symbols were replaced by those originated during the French revolution or the Paris Commune. But over the years many Russian symbols were reintroduced to share the field with the communist ones. Not all the Russian symbols reappeared; neither the imperial eagle nor the old flag did. But Russian military ranks and insignias were restored, and Russia's past victories, even those achieved during the expansion of the Romanov empire, were again glorified.

Revolutionary symbols have been almost thoroughly devalued. The color red, the red star, and the hammer and sickle have lost a great deal of their former luster. Few Soviet men like to buy the red ties so popular in the United States: they look too official, or too much like a child's Pioneer uniform. The inscriptions on the jeans and polo shirts favored by style-conscious young Muscovites are mostly in Latin letters, and well-dressed young girls more often wear small crosses than red stars as pendants.

Revolutionary slogans such as "Peace to the soldier, bread to the worker, land to the peasant" played an essential role in the victory of the Bolshevik revolution. But nowadays official slogans seem to have lost much of their power and are of more interest to Sovietologists than to Soviet citizens. The slogans are supposed to be copied word by word from the newspapers, where they are listed by number in advance of the May First and November Seventh celebrations. Each marching group carries a slogan appropriate to its function. Thus, an academic institution might carry one glorifying higher learning, while a factory group will

Voices

"Since Stalin's time we have had in our blood the formula: 'We thank the Party and the government for our happy life.' It never even occurred to us to think that this formula is basically senseless."

From a discussion in *Literaturnaia gazeta*, June 6, 1988.

carry a slogan exhorting workers to overfulfill that year's production plan. General political slogans can be used by all. With the whole process bureaucratized to the extreme, nobody pays much attention to the texts of the slogans adorning walls and buildings on official holidays. In many cities, permanently installed billboard-style panels bearing various political exhortations have been torn down.

Now that the words *glasnost* (openness) and *perestroika* (restructuring) are internationally recognized and understood, Mikhail Gorbachev may have breathed new life into the political slogan. What will be more interesting, though, is whether Soviet society can develop a language of real political discourse.

28

Soviet Culture

From the very outset of the Soviet regime, the creation of a new culture and a new man was foremost in the minds of the revolutionary leaders. This new culture and new man were supposed to be proletarian in character, rooted in international worker solidarity. The bourgeois and the aristocratic past were rejected, along with their cultural achievements. Such classic Russian writers as Pushkin, Lermontov, and Nekrasov were castigated as the mouthpieces of old social classes, while many great literary works of the non-Russian peoples were considered infected with nationalist sentiment.

Within the limits of a short chapter one can give only a very condensed view of "Soviet culture." Even the question of whether there really is such a thing as Soviet culture, or only separate Russian, Ukrainian, Lithuanian, Uzbek, and other national cultures, is controversial.

Nor is there much "beef" in the concept of the "new Soviet man." One meets no such ideal Soviet man, but rather a variety of Soviet people, differentiated by nationality and social class, not to speak of political and cultural preferences. All of them have indeed acquired some common "Soviet" characteristics: a degree of egalitarianism, a "streetwise" ability to deal with bureaucratic obstacles, and a cynical attitude toward all ideologies. However, the "new Soviet man," a colorless paragon selflessly devoted to social good at the cost of enormous personal sacrifice, is to be met in political folklore and didactic fiction, nowhere else.

The 1920s were a period of great upheaval in Russian literature and culture. The most prominent among the prerevolutionary writers, artists, and painters, from Ivan Bunin to Marc Chagall, shocked by the terror of the civil war and discouraged by postrevolutionary desolation, had left the country by 1920, abandoning the field to younger, less established artists. The latter went through a period of radical experimentation before breaking into competing factions—the independently minded "fellow travelers," the uncommitted "Serapion brothers," the futurists of the LEF (Left Front of Art), the "proletarian writers" of the Proletkult, and the "peasant writers." The New Economic Policy provided an economic foundation for the cultural revival.

An interesting and diversified literature emerged, the creation of poets Esenin and Mayakovsky, novelists Bulgakov and Olesha, humorists Zoshchenko, Ilf and Petrov, short story writers Babel and Ivanov, and many others. However, the spirit of experimentation all but vanished once the Russian Association of Proletarian Writers established a dictatorship in the field of arts, parallel to the one officially exercised in politics by the proletariat. The suicides of two leading figures marked the end of the literary freedom of the 1920s: that of Sergei Esenin, the melodic poet of the Russian village, and that of Vladimir Mayakovsky, the futurist bard of the coming industrial age.

At the same time, however, some of the exiles began to return home. Among them was Maxim Gorky, a leading prerevolutionary writer who was a Bolshevik sympathizer but a humanist made uneasy by revolutionary excesses. His eagerness to protect younger writers and develop their talents, combined with his artistic honesty (he never wrote a single work of fiction dealing with Stalin's Russia), contrasted with his role as a front man for the regime, always ready to affix his signature to the most distasteful propaganda statement.

Although Gorky helped to overthrow the "proletarian dictatorship" in literature, he also played a key role, at the 1934 First Congress of Soviet Writers, in establishing "socialist realism" as the sole authorized current in Soviet literature and culture, with the most painful long-term consequences for Soviet culture. Socialist realism demanded that works of literature and art be involved in "socialist construction" and written with the latter in mind, promoting enthusiasm for the cause and optimism for the future. Anything contrary to the interests of socialism was to be barred. "Neutral" works were rejected as useless.

Socialist realism was based on three main principles, namely *partiinost*, *narodnost*, and *tipichnost*. The first meant a genuine identification with the cause of the party, the second mandated the use of language accessible to the common man, and the third required that the plot be mundane. Realism was to prevail, whether in prose, poetry, music, or art, and all other trends, from modern art to literary formalism, were rejected outright. The one exception was that whenever reality fell short of the socialist ideal (nearly always), the latter was to be depicted. Whereas a realistic description (or painting) of a Soviet slum would be prohibited, a similar work depicting an American slum would be praised: the first shows socialism in a bad light, the second is critical of conditions under capitalism.

Socialist realism became the straitjacket of Soviet culture, a filter through which many works of art could never pass, and a podium for artistically inferior but politically "correct" works. Some talented writers—Alexei Tolstoy and Mikhail Sholokhov, for example—managed to produce works of high quality while remaining subservient to the regime. But the great majority of writers produced a grim sort of "pulp" literature. Other writers and artists simply stopped publishing or exhibiting, or turned to children's stories, translations, and illustrations. Finally, in the late 1930s, many fell victim to the purges. Quite a number of gifted artists vanished in Stalin's camps (Isaak Babel, Osip Mandelshtam) or committed suicide (Marina Tsvetaeva) during those years.

After a short cultural relaxation during World War II (an expedient concession to the need to mobilize the totality of public opinion in support of the regime), socialist realism reasserted

Voices

"The paper souls that feed upon circulars and directives have also extended their clerkish, pencil-pushing views to literature. In their opinion, literature must operate according to certain rules and within a certain framework. But the rest of life, with its diversity and multiple frameworks, is excluded because it is unpleasant or inconvenient or it plays into the hands of the enemy. . . .

I was reprimanded for one of my stories about the war—for supposedly exaggerating, for being too pointed, for distortions. And when I asked 'But isn't that the way it was?' the answer was: 'That is the way it was . . . It happened. That's true. But why write about it?' And [their] reasons seem the most noble: it does not contribute to a patriotic upbringing, it dampens young people's ardor, etc.

To my way of thinking a writer has just one obligation, and that is to tell the truth."

From an interview with Vasil' Bykov,
Literaturnaia gazeta, May 14, 1986

itself and remained in full control until Stalin's death. It is only since then—and especially since the "Thaw," which began after Khrushchev allowed *Novyi mir* to publish Alexander Solzhenitsyn's *One Day in the Life of Ivan Denisovich*—that socialist realism's grip on Soviet cultural life was loosened, allowing for greater freedom of expression.

Still, the persecution of Boris Pasternak for allowing his novel *Doctor Zhivago* to be published abroad cut short the Thaw. After Khrushchev's ouster in 1964, and the arrest, trial, and imprisonment of writers Siniavsky and Daniel in 1965, strict limits on the permitted bounds of artistic expression were again imposed. Respect for old Russian literature returned with vengeance, and the nineteenth-century classics became virtually the sacred cows of Soviet literary critics. The translation of many Western works and the reprinting of unorthodox Soviet literary works of the 1920s slowed down, and modern art exhibits were rare. Not until the late 1980s were Chagall's paintings exhibited, *Zhivago* published, and relative freedom of artistic expression restored.

Under Gorbachev, Soviet culture in all its forms is enjoying the highest level of freedom since the early 1920s, leaving relatively little under restriction, except for works by certain prominent emigrés openly scornful of the Soviet system.

To discuss Soviet culture solely in terms of Moscow and Leningrad circles fails to cover the field. There is a popular culture in the USSR, as anywhere else, a culture of the masses. In that domain Soviet achievements are a mixed bag of successes and failures. On one hand, the cultural level of the average Russian or Tatar or Uzbek has risen tremendously, and there are very few genuine illiterates. Publishing is booming (though not in all the languages of the country), attendance at theaters, movie houses, museums, galleries, and exhibits is excellent. Some truly fine artists from among the non-Russian nationalities are internationally known (the novelist Chingiz Aitmatov, to cite just one outstanding example). Television (a mixed blessing), and of course radio, are universally present, even in the remotest areas. On the reverse side, the intellectual level of nineteenth-century Russian high culture has not been generally maintained. The Russian language has been impoverished by the absorption of bureaucratic jargon, slang, and abbreviations, and the other languages of the country have been similarly affected.

The richness of cultural life contrasts sharply with the poverty of ''night life'' in Soviet cities. Combining dinner in a restaurant with an evening at the theater is almost impossible since nothing is offered after nine o'clock (only hard-currency tourist places stay open). Moreover, obtaining tickets to anything of interest is very difficult: the same queues and shortages that affect shopping plague cultural activities as well.

The cultural life of Moscow and Leningrad is duplicated, albeit on a more modest scale, in provincial centers. Thus many

medium-size cities have their own performing theaters, something one cannot always find in American towns of comparable
size. In the capitals of the union republics the quality of cultural
life varies drastically, depending on tradition and national vitality.

In judging the state of Soviet culture, we often tend to concentrate on past and present restrictions, from censorship to the
outright persecution of nonconformists and dissidents. While not
denying the importance of total artistic freedom and the negative
role played by socialist realism, we must not overlook the positive side—the spread of cultural life into the remotest parts of the
country, involving all levels of the population.

29

The Media

One of the first acts of the Soviet government after the triumph of the October revolution was the establishment of a state monopoly over the media. This state of affairs has never changed. All the newspapers, magazines, and journals, all the publishing houses, and all the radio and television stations in the USSR are directly, or through the intermediary of state-controlled public organizations, controlled by state and party authorities. This situation is not unique to the Soviet Union; with a few minor differences, it exists in all the countries of the ''socialist bloc.''

Control over the media is vested in Glavlit, the Chief Administration for Literary and Publishing Affairs, which covers radio and television programs as well and exercises advance censorship. It is only recently, under *glasnost*, that Glavlit's role has been somewhat curtailed.

In Stalin's time, Procurator General Vyshinsky summed up the official policy on freedom of expression in the following words: ''In our State, there is and can be no place for freedom of speech, press, and so on, for the foes of socialism.'' Article 50 of the Soviet Constitution states the principle this way: ''In accordance with the interests of the people and in order to strengthen and develop the socialist system, citizens of the USSR are guaranteed freedom of speech, of the press, and of assembly, meetings, street processions, and demonstrations. . . .''

With the purpose of freedom of expression clearly defined as being freedom to support the status quo, and with the authorities being the ultimate judge, the Soviet meaning of this freedom takes a very peculiar bend.

Soviet newspapers look quite different from ours. Whereas American newspapers are thick and filled with ads, and present newsworthy stories up front, Soviet newspapers are thin, carry very few if any ads, and hide most of the news on the back pages. Moreover, Soviet papers publish articles on many narrow subjects that we normally reserve for specialized trade journals.

Nationwide newspapers are published in Moscow. There are also newspapers published in the individual republics, as well as regional ones, and finally the local district press. As far as the subject matter is concerned, there are general interest newspapers and others aimed at special audiences such as young people or collective farmers. Journals are generally of two kinds—the weeklies and the monthly "fat journals" of 200–300 pages. The former are mostly of general interest; the latter are usually literary. The journals, with few exceptions, appear only in Moscow and in the other capital cities.

Among the better-known central newspapers are *Pravda*, the official organ of the Central Committee of the Communist Party; *Izvestiia*, the principal government newspaper; and *Komsomol'-skaia pravda*, the newspaper of the Communist Youth League. The best-known weekly magazines are *Ogonek*, an illustrated weekly mixing art, literature, and social issues, and *Krokodil*, a satirical weekly known for its high-quality cartoons. The most popular "fat journals" include the famous *Novyi mir*, *Oktiabr'*, *Znamia*, and the youth monthly *Iunost'*, all literary journals with a leavening of essays dealing with social issues. Among specialized publications, one can mention the Red Army newspaper *Krasnaia zvezda*, the trade union newspaper *Trud*, and the self-explanatory *Sovetskii sport*.

Each republic has its own press, published both in Russian and in the main local language. In the Slavic republics of Ukraine and Belorussia, as well as in Kazakhstan and Kirgizia (which have large Russian populations), the Russian-language press predominates. But in all other union republics, and in many autonomous ones, the reverse is true. Regions and districts have their own newspapers, but the latter tend to be even thinner than the republican ones and contain a large number of articles simply reprinted from either the republican or the central press. The central papers tend to have six to eight pages, the republican four to six, and the regional about four. District newspapers usually have about four pages in a smaller format and appear three times a week instead of six.

But it is not the number and the size of these publications, or their variety, that is peculiar to the Soviet press. It is rather the political conformity, the linguistic uniformity, and the boring content that set it apart from the "capitalist press."

During Stalin's era and other periods of repression, political conformity has, indeed, been total. But whenever some relaxation takes place, individual editors manage to show some variety of political inclinations within the newly enlarged limits. Not counting the period prior to the consolidation of Stalin's dictatorship, there have been two (or rather two-and-a-half) periods of relative relaxation, the "half" taking place during World War II.

Spurred by the need to secure the widest popular backing for the war effort, the regime found it necessary to court such previously despised groups as world Jewry, the Russian Orthodox church, and the offspring of liquidated social classes ranging from kulaks to nobles. Accordingly, the Soviet media showed a much more favorable attitude toward these groups. After the war, although Jews definitely fell from political favor, the more tolerant attitude toward the church was sustained, and citizens with "wrong" social origin were no longer actively harassed for the "sins" of their parents.

The second and much more serious relaxation came in 1955–56. Known as the "Thaw," it followed upon Khrushchev's 1956 "secret speech" denouncing Stalin's crimes. It lasted, with its ups and downs, for roughly a decade, and slowly vanished during the first years of Brezhnev's rule. During the Thaw, several literary publications took a much more liberal stand than the rest of the Soviet press. In the forefront were the "fat journal" *Novyi mir*, the youth journal *Iunost'*, the weekly *Literaturnaia gazeta*,

Voices

"When international reporters talk about elucidating the internal life of foreign countries . . . the term 'balanced information' is widely used; that is, a certain weighing and balancing of positive and negative points, in the interest of objectivity. In practice, though, this is often understood in the following way: one segment on electronic cow husbandry in Holland to one hundred reports on the troubles of the unemployed and homeless in America."

Izvestiia reporter Stanislav N. Kondrashov
in *Kommunist*, 1987, no. 14

as well as some newly appearing literary almanacs. At the end of the Thaw, the editors-in-chief of all the "liberal" publications were replaced and their staffs purged. The guilty recanted, and everything returned to the normal state of conformity. Risky works found refuge in *samizdat* (self-publication) or even *tamizdat* ("there," or foreign, publication).

A new liberalization has begun since the advent of Gorbachev, roughly two decades after the demise of Khrushchev's "Thaw." It is without doubt the most far-reaching liberalization of the Soviet media we have ever seen. On the forefront of the new trend are the newspapers *Izvestiia*, *Komsomol'skaia pravda*, and *Moscow News* (which appears in Russian and in foreign-language editions), the weekly newspaper *Sovetskaia kul'tura*, and above all, the weekly magazine *Ogonek*. The case of *Ogonek* is especially striking. With the appointment of a new editor-in-chief, V. A. Korotych, this formerly colorless publication, known for its unimaginative content, underwent a startling transformation. It became the most open mass-circulation publication in the country as a whole, critically investigative, and willing to tackle almost any

Voices

"Right now we speak freely about everything, but I sometimes think: what if the process of democratization comes to a stop? The first thing that will happen, some big party functionary who dreams about the dictatorship of the party . . . will try to strangle *glasnost*."

From a discussion in *Literaturnaia gazeta*, June 6, 1988

subject. Whereas in the past, copies of *Ogonek* piled up unsold on newsstand counters, today the magazine sells out within minutes after reaching the stands.

In some of the union republics highly outspoken publications have also appeared. For example, in Estonia, the monthly journal of the Communist Youth League, *Raduga* (which appears in a larger Estonian and a smaller Russian-language version), seems as determined as *Ogonek* to test the limits of *glasnost*.

Besides the problem of elbow room for the press, there is also the problem of Soviet journalistic lingo, which has infected the Soviet media. The language of Soviet publications acquired a texture that is difficult to explain to anyone who has never read them. It resembles a kind of linguistic mixture of political sloganeering and trade-letter writing for something like the ball-bearing or dairy products industry. Standard sentences abound. Nouns tend to be paired with the same adjectives, and verbs followed by same nouns, and repeated *ad infinitum*, turning reading into a severe test of the reader's resistance to boredom. It is only during periods of relaxation, like the one we are seeing at this moment, that better publications shed this "wooden language" and become readable, some of them even highly so. If this were the sole accomplishment of the Gorbachev administration, it would be enough to give him a place in literary history.

Soviet radio and television stations are all run by governmental agencies. Differences between stations do exist, however, and become more evident in times of political relaxation. First of all, there are substantial differences in the media of different republics, as surfaced when the personnel of Armenian television insisted upon showing the demonstrations in the city of Erevan demanding the transfer of Nagorno-Karabakh to Armenia. The Estonian television network is also known to be more outspoken than many others in its broadcasts. The fact that northern Estonia can pick up Finnish television programs helps in the matter: what is the point of withholding news from people who can readily learn about it elsewhere?

Watching Soviet television programs at this moment is much more entertaining than it was a few years ago, although the programs are still not uncensored. Thus the Soviet press, radio, and television managed to omit such embarrassing items as U.N. votes demanding Soviet withdrawal from Afghanistan, or the international outcry over the downing of the Korean airliner. Until recently buying a foreign noncommunist newspaper in any language was virtually impossible except in the most exclusive Intourist hotels.

Foreign short-wave broadcasts beamed in Russian and in other languages of the Soviet Union by American, English, and Western European stations were jammed for years, but this seemed to have ceased in the late 1980s. Most striking is the fact that the USA–USSR TV satellite bridge programs have been transmitted verbatim on Soviet television, allowing listeners to hear opinions never before publicly expressed in their own country. Whether this is the highpoint of *glasnost*, or just the beginning, only time will tell.

30

The Multicultural Dimension

Lenin's nationalities policy was substantially more favorable to non-Russians than tsarist policy had been: national discrimination was outlawed, Russian chauvinism was brought under control, and the use of local languages was supported. However, once Lenin became ill, it was Stalin who set out the bases of Soviet nationalities policy.

In the cultural realm, Stalin put into practice the formula "national in form, socialist in content." What this really meant was limiting the role of "national" components of culture to the language itself and to cultural creations of a purely folkloric character, such as folk dances. Moscow was to control everything else. Thus, where literature and the arts were concerned, socialist realism was in, and national epics and works showing evidence of religious or nationalist feeling were out.

Language problems were and remain a sore point in Soviet nationalities policy. With Russian being quite legitimately "the language of communication" among the nationalities of the country, the role of other languages and the place of bilingualism are hot issues. It is obvious that a decent command of Russian is required to work, study, and socialize beyond one's own group. But the problem is aggravated by the reluctance on the part of Russian settlers in the other republics to learn the local language, creating a situation in which bilingualism is a one-way street.

The *korenizatsiia* policy in the 1920s, which required non-local officials to learn the language of the republic where they

Books and Brochures Published in Various Languages

Language	1960		1986	
	No. of titles	Print run (in 000)	No. of titles	Print run (in 000)
Russian	55,337	1,016,356	64,001	1,914,055
Ukrainian	3,852	80,580	1,828	76,299
Belorussian	430	7,372	383	6,045
Uzbek	1,060	15,524	955	27,438
Georgian	1,889	9,695	1,764	20,408
Lithuanian	1,773	11,367	2,039	20,082

Source: Narodnoe khoziaistvo SSSR v tsifrakh (Moscow, 1987).

were employed, was of short duration. In many instances Russian officials, including the highest ones, not only neglect to learn the local language, but, being themselves ''parachuted'' into the area, have minimal knowledge, interest, or ties in the given republic. Compulsory study of local languages in the Russian-language schools established on the territory of many republics failed to survive as well. Moreover, in places where it did survive, few Russian students took it seriously enough to reach any degree of fluency.

Stalin's language policy was also marked by a meddling with alphabets. Initially, the written languages of the Muslim peoples of the USSR were changed from the Arabic to the Latin alphabet (a move followed by Turkey shortly afterward). One side effect of this change was to make the Koran less accessible. Later, another shift took place. This time the same languages were transferred to the Cyrillic alphabet used for writing Russian. This was a purely political measure, for Russification purposes.

Publications in non-Russian languages, strongly promoted after the revolution, underwent a very uneven evolution. Until roughly 1960, there was an increase in publications for almost all of them, then a decrease for Ukrainian and Belorussian, but continued growth for publishing in Uzbek, Georgian, Estonian, and Lithuanian.

Stalin also put his stamp on the terminology of national relations. He developed a three-stage formula describing the desired
developmental sequence. The first stage would bring a flourish-
ing (*rastsvet*) of individual nationalities under socialist conditions, followed by a process of rapprochement (*sblizhenie*)
among nationalities as they developed more commonalities. The
final stage would bring a fusion (*sliianie*) of all Soviet nationalities in the future communist society. This last stage has been
subsequently redefined a number of times to make it less offensive to the national minorities, who rightfully perceive "fusion"
as a Russian melting pot in which non-Russian nationalities are to
be dissolved. For that matter, many Russians view fusion of all
the peoples of the Soviet Union as potentially threatening to the
preservation of their own Russian national and cultural identity.

The emphasis on the "big brother" role of the Russian people
is another component of the same terminology. This was totally
absent in Lenin's day; colonial conquests, Russian included,
were condemned. When Stalin, in the 1930s, proclaimed the
progressive character of Russian conquests, whether tsarist or
not, Russia was adorned with the "big brother" distinction,
leading its junior partners on the road to communism. This theme
has vanished of late, to be replaced by one of cooperation among
nationalities.

The resurgence of nationalist movements since the mid-1980s
belies decades of official satisfaction with the "solution" of the
nationalities problem.

By and large the Muslims, most of whom live in six union
republics (Uzbekistan, Kazakhstan, Azerbaijan, Tajikistan, Turkmenistan, and Kirgizia) and in five autonomous republics of the
RSFSR (the Tatar, Bashkir, Checheno-Ingush, Dagestan, and Ka-
bardino-Balkar ASSRs) constitute the least assimilable element
among Soviet nationalities. Too many things keep them apart
from the rest: religion, culture, language, way of life. The Soviet
Muslims are mostly Turkic-speaking and of the Sunni branch of

Voices

"Do all the Russians understand that the constant use of the expression 'Great Russian People' indirectly belittles the other nations of our country?"

"The first and foremost problem of a genuine policy of democratization of society . . . is one of fulfillment of really guaranteed conditions for an unhindered existence and development of national cultures, for the development of nations in their totality. As long as this problem is not addressed (especially in a multinational country like the USSR), as long as it is not democratically handled, it is useless to talk about the progress of democratization."

"For a long time [the national spirit] was always branded as nothing other than 'a survival of the bourgeois past,' 'an ideological diversion,' etc., in Estonia, in Russia, and in Kazakhstan. In the era of *glasnost*, even the political leadership must realize that the national question cannot be solved by decrees or by the [state] security organs. The only road toward solving that problem is inseparable from the national spirit, which remains its foundation."

"Bureaucratic, chauvinist, and nihilist lawlessness, cultivated for a long time, wrought enormous damage to the national languages and the historic souls of some nations. It will be impossible to implement national justice without making reparations."

From *Raduga*, the journal of the Young Communist
League of Estonia, Nos. 1 and 4, 1988

Islam, exceptions being the Iranian-speaking Tajiks and the Shiite Azerbaijani. Like other groups they tend to comply with the official rules of the game, join the party, and proclaim their allegiance to socialism. But in everyday life, marital and family customs, work preferences, and social habits their value system is Muslim, Middle Eastern, Oriental, and not European or Slavic.

Even the most Russified among Soviet Muslims, those fluent in Russian, married to Russian women (the reverse is rare, being forbidden by the Shariat, or Islamic religious law), and occupying important positions in their own republics, tend to share Russian values only to an extent, are often casually indifferent to communist dogma, and view their own integration in Russian-dominated Soviet society more in terms of a comfortable arrangement than as genuine adhesion to a basically alien set of values. This is one reason why the demographic boom in Muslim areas causes a great deal of concern in Moscow.

The two Christian republics of Transcaucasia present a different set of problems. First of all, Georgians and Armenians feel very little kinship for each other (and even less for their Muslim neighbors in Azerbaijan). They are ancient nations, Christian since the fourth century, with strong cultural traditions. The educational level in both Georgia and Armenia is higher than in Russia, and so is the standard of living. Thus anti-Russian sentiments are rare there, despite a great deal of national pride, sometimes bruised by Moscow. For Georgians and Armenians, Christian Russia has always been a lesser evil in comparison to Turkish or Iranian Muslim domination.

Georgians glory in their noble past, when their nobility was proportionately as numerous as that in eighteenth-century Poland. Even today, one Georgian prince living in the republic is proudly introduced by his title. Stalin is still revered there, not so much for his deeds (Georgians suffered from his abuses as much as other nationalities), but for the fact of his having ruled Russia, an achievement comparable to the Corsican Napoleon becoming the Emperor of France.

Armenians, on the other hand, are more of a mercantile nation. No titles of nobility survived there. Prior to the revolution, Armenians were active in commerce all over the Caucasus and

Central Asia, and even in Russia proper. They are still active, not only in commerce but in science and industry as well. Nationalist feeling in Armenia today may be as high as it was decades ago, but it is still primarily directed against Armenia's Turkic-speaking neighbors and not against Moscow.

The three Baltic republics are a case apart. All three gained independence from Russia after the October revolution and remained independent until World War II. Annexed by the USSR in 1940, they were occupied by the Germans in the summer of 1941, liberated by the Russians in 1944, and have remained in Moscow's hands since then. Many citizens of those republics fell victim to Stalin and Hitler terror: some fled to Sweden and beyond, others were repressed during the collectivization drive of the early 1950s. National pride in the republics is very strong, local language and culture is respected, and unbridled Russian immigration is perceived as a threat to the national character of the area.

Today, Estonia, Lithuania, and Latvia (in that order) enjoy the highest standard of living in the country as well as the best quality of life. These conditions attract many unwanted immigrants, especially to labor-short Estonia and Latvia. Among the demands the Baltic republics are making today are for tighter immigration controls, economic autonomy, free trade zones, and compulsory study of local languages by nonnative officials and in nonnative schools. But despite the strength of local national feelings and the new assertiveness of republic officials, the Baltic peoples are numerically too weak to present a challenge to the country's stability. Moreover, the Russians do respect the cultural level and thriving work ethic of this most ''Western'' region of the country. For these reasons Moscow has, so far at least, abstained from clamping down on the Baltic republics.

Soviet Moldavians in fact do not constitute a separate nationality, but are a branch of the Romanian people and speak the same language.

The Soviet north is a special case, having more in common with the problems of the Canadian north than with the national situation elsewhere in the USSR. Here Soviet policy has been basically benevolent: local national groups have been helped along the road to progress and modernization. It is probably the region where the Soviet nationalities policy has been most successful, largely due to the unlikelihood of any conceivable threat coming from so small and dispersed a population.

Russia's "sister" republics are another special case. The degree of national identification is very uneven in both Ukraine and Belorussia: strong in the west (in formerly Polish areas), moderate from there to Kiev, and weak in the east and on the Black Sea coast. The Ukrainian and Belorussian languages are both on the retreat, and this has caused some concern, especially among Ukrainian nationalists. The question is whether the decline of the Ukrainian language and the rapid erosion of Belorussian are caused by Moscow's policies or rather by the natural inroads of the Russian language and culture.

Given the high degree of social and personal acceptance among individuals from the three Slavic nations, their cultural similarities and easy intermarriage, the real extent of Ukrainian and Belorussian nationalist feelings remains an open question.

There is also another dimension to the problem. Ukrainians and Belorussians, unlike most other national minority groups in the Soviet Union today, occupy a full share of top federal positions along with Russians and are readily substituted for Russians in staffing key control positions in the Muslim and Baltic republics as well. In the face of growing Muslim numbers and of nationalist feelings all over the country, Moscow does its best to keep Ukrainians and Belorussians content: together they can face any emergency in the years to come.

31

Religion

Virtually every religion is represented in the Soviet Union—Eastern Orthodoxy, Roman Catholicism, and Protestantism, Islam in both Sunni and Shiite versions, Judaism, and Buddhism. Officially, of course, the country is atheistic, but different religions are tolerated to various degrees at different times.

Marx's view that "Religion is the opium of the people" was the original justification for Soviet policies restricting the practice of religion. An underlying reason for these policies, however, was the fact that communist ideology itself is quasi-religious in character, demanding total commitment for the sake of a remote communist paradise to be enjoyed by future generations, much the way some religions promise rewards in an afterlife for those who follow certain precepts on this earth.

Like any new faith, at the outset Soviet communist ideology was intolerant of all competition, but it mellowed with age. Up until World War II the regime was very hostile toward organized religion. Many priests and mullahs were arrested and deported. Churches, mosques, and synagogues were closed, or transformed into clubs, galleries, depots, grain bins, offices, and even stables. Books of religious content were no longer printed or permitted to be imported from abroad. The teaching of Hebrew was prohibited. Attending religious services was dangerous for working-age people and their children; the only ones who could do so without fear of serious consequences were elderly people, whom the regime wrote off as the dying remnants of the old society, with no role to play in modern times.

Voices

"Conscience, compassion, and mercy are moral principles that have been affirmed in the human world from century to century. Along with the dark sides, which provided grounds for considering religion 'the opium of the people,' religion has also espoused universal human values that are important for all times and all nations. When the struggle against religion was launched during the first years . . . certain zealots immediately began rejecting everything out of hand . . . but how can one renounce everything that his been nurtured by centuries of a people's ethics, spirituality, and morality?"

From an interview with Vasil' Bykov,
Literaturnaia gazeta, May 14, 1986

During the same period, scores of ancient Russian churches were demolished by eager "renovators." Even St. Basil's Cathedral on Red Square barely escaped demolition. National treasures destroyed during that period are irreplaceable, and their loss is a source of lament in the Soviet press today. It is worth noting that at this moment the Romanian Communist leader Ceausescu proposes to demolish an ancient Bucharest cathedral to enlarge his parade grounds. In Gorbachev's USSR this would be unthinkable.

During the 1920s and 1930s priests and monks were branded as parasites profiting from public ignorance. Everything possible was done to paint them as morally derelict. Graves with skeletons of newborn babies were supposedly discovered near convents, dog bones were allegedly found in the tombs of saints, gold and foreign currency in monasteries. Priests were charged with drunkenness, debauchery, and larceny. Believers were pictured as ranging from senile elders to former exploiters. Sportive, clean-cut, healthy young communist youths were shown confronting priests of degenerate and foul aspect. Antireligious societies flourished, actively supported by the party and the state.

World War II produced an enormous change. Faced with the German onslaught, Stalin saw the urgent need to rally Russian public opinion to the defense of the fatherland. To this end, the support of the Russian Orthodox church, still rich in both open and hidden believers, was a necessity. As a result, and almost overnight, the church was lifted from its pariah status to one of relative tolerance. Personal attacks against clergymen ceased, and many among those who had been forced to abandon the pulpit were allowed to resume their functions. Priests were freed from the camps, and a few churches were allowed to reopen.

Since it was impolitic to show tolerance for Russian Orthodoxy without similar indulgence toward other major religions, all faiths were granted more recognition than before. Stalin assidu-ously courted international support among Jews during the war. Four Muslim religious directorates were established (three Sun-ni, one Shiite), patterned after institutions that originated during the reign of Catherine the Great. Officially registered Muslim clergy were allowed to function within strictly established limits in the surviving mosques.

The increased tolerance for Russian Orthodoxy and Islam did not carry over to the Roman Catholic church or to the Uniate church, which recognizes the Pope. The Uniates, based mostly in western Ukraine, were subjected to heavy persecution follow-ing the liberation of the area from German occupation. The jailing of Uniate clergymen, forced dissolution of the church itself, and "reconversion" of its faithful to Russian Ortho-doxy were painful episodes. Similarly, tolerance of "offi-cial" Islam failed to protect the Muslim clergy and the mosques of the seven small "punished peoples" deported by Stalin during the war. As for the Jews, shortly before his death Stalin was engaged in launching the first stages of an antisemitic campaign.

The post-Stalin years saw a slow improvement in the status of the Orthodox church and of Islam and increased leeway for the Armenian and Georgian churches. The Muslim groups allowed to return home were also permitted to reopen the few mosques operational prior to the war, and to rehabilitate a few more. On the other hand, the positions of Catholicism and of Judaism deteriorated, probably because of their Western orientation. There were no more than sixty to seventy functioning synagogues in the USSR in the mid-1960s. Where Protestants are concerned, the Lutheran church in Estonia was tolerated, mostly because of its limited influence, but the Protestant sects that began to flourish among the Russians in the 1960s and 1970s were given a hard time. They were seen as both fanatical and linked to America. Although the Muslims, too, have external ties, their sheer numbers (over 50 million in the USSR), as well as the role of Islam in the international arena, make wholesale repression inadvisable.

Antireligious propaganda during the post-Stalin years remained rather primitive. Yuri Gagarin, the first Soviet cosmonaut, was said not to have seen God in outer space. The journal *Science and Religion* continued its usual attacks on religious rituals, clergy, and faith. In some areas of the country the most superstitious manifestations of religious belief were better tolerated than established religions, whose churches and mosques remain closed. Obviously it was considered good tactics to show religion in an unappealing, primitive light.

Security agents have penetrated the religious hierarchy of the Russian Orthodox church and, to a lesser extent, of other denominations as well. Overly zealous Orthodox priests have routinely been reprimanded by their church superiors. Moreover, seminary study was not facilitated, except perhaps in the case of the Armenian church. For Sunni Muslims there are only two institutions, each with a very limited enrollment: one (higher) in Tashkent, another (lower) in Bukhara. The *medresseh* in Bukhara has a student body of about fifty, although it receives fifty applications for each space. An active unofficial Muslim clergy and Sufi brotherhoods fill the vacuum left by the limitations imposed on the official faith. Russian Orthodox seminaries are in somewhat better shape, but Jews and Catholics were permitted only to send a few candidates each year to study in neighboring Eastern European countries. Plans for the opening of a yeshiva in Moscow were announced in early 1989.

The observance of the thousandth anniversary of Christianity in Russia in 1988, combined with Gorbachev's policy of *glasnost*, is bringing more religious tolerance, especially for the Russian Orthodox church, which is increasingly seen by the authorities as essentially patriotic and cooperative. The church is about to recover some long-abandoned properties, and attendance at services by working-age nonparty members is increasingly tolerated. This religious revival in the Slavic areas of the country is connected with several factors:

• the growth of Russian and Ukrainian national self-consciousness, which enhances their religious past and gives present-day Orthodoxy greater respectability;

• Gorbachev's policy of liberalization, which makes church attendance less risky for working-age people;

• the increasing attraction of Soviet youth to religious symbolism and the beauty of church architecture, chants, and music. Even if this attraction is not turning young people into believers, it instills a great deal of respect for the church as an institution of historical importance and aesthetic value.

For other groups, the situation is as follows:

• among Soviet Muslims, religion and way of life have remained so intertwined that official attempts to separate the two have consistently failed;

• among Soviet Jews, including many who are nonbelievers, heightened national consciousness has created a level of respect for religion unmatched since prerevolutionary times;

• among the Catholics of Lithuania and southern Latvia, in a situation somewhat similar to that in Poland, the church is seen as the repository of national values and as such has remained invulnerable despite years of repression. The Lithuanian Catholic church includes a cardinal whose name was never published by the Vatican, in order not to aggravate the difficulties between the Lithuanian church and the Soviet authorities. A Latvian cardinal was named in 1988;

• the Armenian and Georgian churches, which enjoyed more freedom than others even before the current liberalization, continue to be favored. The Catholics of Armenia and the patriarch of Georgia are given more leeway than their Russian counterparts. In Armenia, the number of working-age worshipers is especially high, and the authorities try to impress the world Armenian community with the degree of religious freedom enjoyed by the Soviet Armenian population.

In summary, the various religions of the Soviet Union, despite two decades of harsh persecution (1920s and 1930s), two subsequent decades of very limited tolerance (1940s and 1950s), and two decades of restrictions (1960s and 1970s), have managed to emerge in the 1980s with a respectable proportion of believers and a barely tarnished prestige among the population. Years of antireligious propaganda did little to weaken the attraction of religion; the general modernization of the society did, but this would have taken place regardless of any antireligious effort on the part of the authorities. To the contrary, the intensity of repression has probably strengthened, not weakened, the faith of the remaining believers.

32

Dissent

Dissent in the Soviet Union is a very complex subject, for dissent can have many grounds—cultural, religious, national, or purely political. Moreover, different dissenters' programs can be incompatible and even antithetical. The cause of Armenian nationalists in Nagorno-Karabakh has little in common with that of Russophile historians or those advocating the publication of Alexander Solzhenitsyn's works. Still, within the restrictive confines of a dogmatic system, any sort of disagreement with accepted truths and values can be seen as dissent, and treated accordingly.

Under Stalin, when something as trivial as an anecdote overheard by an inappropriate person could pave the way to a concentration camp, one could not expect much defiance. Among Soviet writers it is probably the late Ilya Ehrenburg who best explained the fear paralyzing Soviet intellectuals; he himself was an excellent example of that condition, kowtowing to Stalin during the latter's life and revealing his true feelings only afterward.

The only prudent course during the Stalin era was to remain as uninvolved as possible: attend meetings without taking part in them, vote for whatever was proposed and whoever was the candidate, and diligently study Stalin's "bible," the *Short History of the Communist Party of the Soviet Union*, by repeating standard sentences in unison with other co-workers. The waves of deportees in the 1930s and 1940s were not made up of real counterrevolutionaries but of those whom the leader perceived as potential dissenters. Some were even less than that: unlucky by-standers caught in the web of collective responsibility.

Open dissent appeared only after Stalin's death and can be divided into four major categories of causes: human rights, intellectual, nationalist, and religious. The major dissident groups are:

- human rights activists;
- intellectuals struggling for freedom of expression;
- nationalist dissenters, naturally including a number of sub-groups:

—Jews searching for Jewish cultural roots, or seeking to emigrate;

—Germans seeking to emigrate;

—Crimean Tatars demanding the right to return to their former homeland from their current diaspora in Central Asia;

—Baltic groups demanding real national autonomy and a review of official interpretations of their annexation by the Soviet Union;

—Ukrainians who seek to preserve their cultural and linguistic distinctiveness;

—Russian nationalists, ranging from moderates to reactionaries, calling for a return to "eternal Russian values";

- religious activists, again subdivided into several groups but including, among others:

—Russian (or Ukrainian) Orthodox clergy, seeking more freedom for the church and less dependence on state authorities;

—members of various small Protestant communities seeking freedom of worship and way of life;

—Muslim Sufi brotherhoods seeking to function without official interference in their activities.

Each group has had phases of particularly heightened activity. Thus the decade 1955–65 was especially characterized by growing intellectual demands, the next decade (1965–75) by increased concern for human rights and for nationalist causes, and the next (1975–85) by a flurry of religious dissent. The post–1985 years are again characterized by growing nationalist activity.

It was Khrushchev's "Thaw" that first unlocked the door to open dissent. The reasons were multifold: the death of Stalin and the subsequent denunciation of his abuses of power, the diminution of fear, and lesser penalties for transgressions (getting fired, rather than the firing squad).

The first dissenters were intellectuals who had joined the de-Stalinization drive but soon found themselves ahead of the pack and beyond the official limits. They saw the doors of literary journals slammed in their faces and turned to *samizdat* (self-publishing). Because they used regular typewriters, making a few carbon copies of each text, strictly speaking they were not engaged in illegal publishing. Nevertheless the authorities, under a variety of pretexts, began to persecute samizdat authors. Some turned to *tamizdat* (publishing abroad), transmitting their manuscripts through foreign intermediaries. The most notorious case of tamizdat was the publication in Italy of Boris Pasternak's *Doctor Zhivago*, a case that provoked hysteria among the official establishment, especially when the author won a Nobel Prize. In 1965 writers Siniavsky and Daniel were tried and imprisoned for publishing abroad under pseudonyms. Nevertheless, the rapid development of tamizdat continued, culminating with the expulsions of Alexander Solzhenitsyn and of Alexander Zinoviev (in 1973 and 1978, respectively), the most notorious and active "dissident writers."

The next stage of dissent is closely connected with the Jewish question. Dormant since the happy ending of the so-called "doctors' plot," when Stalin's timely death put an end to the threat of mass deportations, the Jewish problem reemerged with the Israeli victory in the Six-Day War of 1967. Russian Jewry, having acquired a new sense of pride and a renewed interest in their heritage, became less willing to tolerate growing discrimination. Confronted with official refusal to accommodate Jewish cultural needs, and an "anti-Zionist" campaign that only camouflaged continuing patterns of discrimination, many Jews began to see emigration as the only solution, something unheard of in the Soviet Union since the early 1920s. They were helped by Brezhnev's desire to improve relations with the United States, where there was strong support for the "refuseniks'" cause, and by the tacit support on the part of Russians who were either not against the idea of getting rid of some Jews or simply wanted their jobs or apartments.

The Jewish example encouraged other national groups to follow suit. Thus, Volga Germans, deported to Central Asia and Kazakhstan during World War II, began to seek the right to emigrate to the Federal Republic of Germany. Armenians, some of whom had returned to Soviet Armenia from France after World War II, disillusioned in their turn, joined the quest.

Jewish dissenters were not limited to their own cause. They were often deeply involved in the human rights movement, literary liberalization, the search for religious freedom, and even the protection of the Russian historical heritage. This distinguished the Jewish movement from other national movements, which were more exclusively preoccupied with their own affairs.

Another special case is that of the Crimean Tatars, which attracted a great deal of support from the human rights movement, including such prestigious figures as Andrei Sakharov and (before his expulsion from the USSR) the late General Petro Grigorenko, a Ukrainian.

Of all the dissenting groups, Russian nationalists have been better tolerated by the authorities than any other. Their dissent has focused on two issues: preservation of Russia's historic past (churches, monasteries, and other landmarks); and renewed interest in the traditional Russian village life so damaged by the collectivization of agriculture. Russian nationalists occupy a wide political spectrum, from honest patriots worried about their national heritage and moral values to the chauvinists of the Pamiat Society, hostile to all *inorodtsy*, or "alien" groups (Muslims, Jews, Gypsies, and so forth).

Some of them blame the destruction of many Russian architectural marvels during the 1930s on Stalin's henchman, Lazar Kaganovich, "the father" of the Moscow subway and the lone Jew in Stalin's close circle. The bloody excesses of the early revolutionary years are similarly ascribed to non-Russian officers (Poles, Latvians, Jews) in the Cheka. Today's Russia is pictured as selflessly helping all the nations of the Soviet Union and the Communist bloc at the expense of her own welfare and best interests.

Stories and essays published in such "fat" journals as *Sovremennik* and *Molodaia gvardiia*, as well as in the progressive *Ogonek*, deplore the destruction of churches, the spoiling of nature, and the loss of moral values. The collectivization era is realistically depicted and the fate of the Russian peasantry deplored. But while *Ogonek* blames the leaders of the pre-Gorbachev past, others tend to lay all the blame on those non-Russians who were at times involved in carrying out such policies, holding "alien elements" responsible for Russia's own misfortunes.

In short, while Gorbachev's policies of *glasnost* and liberalization have made more vocal dissidence possible in the USSR today, it would be a great mistake to assume that every dissenter favors the liberalization, democratization, and modernization of Soviet society.

33

Emigration

The whole idea of freedom of movement has been alien to the Russian way of thinking since tsarist times. In medieval Europe the free movement of people across borders was facilitated by the Latin *lingua franca* and by the universality of the Catholic church. But Russia was cut off from all this, and life beyond its borders appeared alien, unholy, and dangerous. All the inhabitants of the realm were supposed to be the property of the ruler, just as serfs were the property of their masters. They were not permitted to depart without authorization—especially abroad, to countries populated by enemies of Orthodox Russia. It is only in the last quarter of the eighteenth century, during Catherine the Great's rule, that Russian nobles received the right to travel abroad without special permission. Commoners had to wait many more years, and serfs were obviously not free to move at all, even inside the country, until their liberation in 1862.

Russians did migrate across the country, both prior to the Mongol invasion and during the conquest of Siberia in the seventeenth century. But Russian migrations never created anything similar to New England, New France, or New Spain. The opportunity for this was in Alaska, an aborted experiment in overseas colonization, but the territory was sold to the United States for less than two cents an acre in 1867.

It is only within the last quarter of the nineteenth century that a large-scale migration of Russian subjects took place, mainly to the United States. But most of these emigrants were not Russians but Jews, and Russian authorities were eager to get rid of them. Ukrainians, who also took part in the migration to the United States and to Canada, came mostly from Galicia, until 1918 a part of the Habsburg empire.

During the civil war a very large exodus took place. "White" emigrants were most often former members of the Russian nobility, wealthy merchants, officers, Cossacks, and intellectuals. They fled with the remnants of the White armies, many by way of Istanbul to Paris and Berlin, less often to the United States.

After the end of the civil war, the freedom of exit lasted more or less until Lenin's death, but it was progressively curtailed in the late 1920s. The door was pushed open again in World War II, when western parts of the European USSR were occupied by the invading German army. Many Soviet soldiers were made prisoners of war, and numerous civilians were deported for work in German factories. Some followed the Germans in retreat. Many of these people, including the soldiers who had joined the so-called Vlasov army under German sponsorship, were forcibly repatriated to the USSR after the war, where they were received as traitors and punished accordingly.

Legal mass departures from the USSR took place three times during the 1940s: in 1940, when as a result of the Molotov-Ribbentrop agreement, Germans living in the annexed Baltic territories were allowed to depart for Germany; in 1943, when Polish soldiers and their families led by General Anders departed to Iran to join British forces; and in 1945–46, when the rest of the Polish deportees and refugees in the Soviet Union were allowed to return to Poland. In 1956 this opportunity was extended to the remaining Poles.

Thereafter, all emigration stopped for another dozen years until it was renewed by Brezhnev in the 1970s, peaking in 1979. This time the emigrés were Jews, Germans, and Armenians (the latter from among those who returned to Armenia after World War II). This wave of limited emigration died off, victim of the downturn in Soviet–American relations after the Soviet invasion of Afghanistan, but has resumed in strength since 1987.

If we take a look at emigration to the United States, we can distinguish four separate waves:

• the massive Jewish/Ukrainian emigration of the late nineteenth and early twentieth centuries. Jewish immigrants were predominantly *shtetl* (ghetto) Jews, literate only in Yiddish; the Ukrainians were mostly illiterate peasants. These immigrants started at the bottom of American society and typically were snubbed by the groups that had already "arrived." It took them, on the average, two generations to "make it." Many among the Jews became involved in labor and socialist causes, and a few even returned to the Soviet Union during the depression. But their grandchildren generally had little attachment to the "old country," which after all was more a stepmother than a mother to them. The Ukrainians, while also undergoing speedy assimilation, seem to have maintained their old ties longer.

• the "White Russian" emigration. This group, which reached Paris and Berlin in the early 1920s, tended to stay in Europe. Only a small part crossed the ocean prior to World War II. During the war more came, escaping mostly from occupied France. This was by and large an educated group, the cream of old Russian society, often titled and fluent in several foreign languages. After initial hardships, they managed to integrate themselves very well, whether in Paris or New York. Except for a few romantic souls, mesmerized by Russia's victories against Hitler, few ever returned to the Soviet Union.

• post–World War II DPs (displaced persons). Branded by Moscow as traitors, these people had good reason to turn west rather than east after the war. A great many of them moved to the United States in the late 1940s. The group contained a variety of elements: genuine Nazi collaborators, victims of Stalin who were glad to escape his rule, and apolitical people whose lives had been disrupted by wartime dislocations. Mostly Slavic (Russian, Ukrainian, Belorussian), this category also includes some North Caucasians and even Central Asians (from among prisoners of war). There were, obviously, very few Jews among them, since the DPs had been on Nazi territory prior to the end of the war. The cultural level of the DPs was varied, but the semi-educated prevailed. They reflected their own time and place. They were no longer the illiterate masses of the turn of the century, not yet the Soviet professionals of the 1970s and 1980s. Although they generally started low on the American social ladder, many reached the middle class.

• the predominantly Jewish emigration of the 1970s. This group (which included non-Jewish spouses) numbered some 270,000, half of whom eventually came to the United States while others settled in Israel. Among other emigrants: ethnic Germans who moved to West Germany and Armenians bound for France or the United States. The latest, Gorbachev-era emigration numbered about 20,000 Germans, 15,000 Armenians, and 10,000 Jews in 1987; and these numbers probably doubled in 1988. Out of that total approximately three-quarters of the Jews and Armenians have come to the United States.

These newcomers are Soviet-educated, predominantly professionals with middle-class aspirations. Their motives for leaving the USSR are many: flight from discrimination, the search for ethnic roots, a longing for more freedom of initiative, travel, and self-fulfillment in general.

The majority are not disappointed despite language difficulties (few know English well enough) and the problem of living in an open society, where so much depends on one's own initiative. The number who return to the USSR has been relatively small: less than 0.5 percent, as against approximately 30 percent on average for all immigrants coming to the United States. But culturally, at least for the time being, the new immigrants remain attached to Russian language, literature, entertainment, food, and social patterns. Many are now taking advantage of Gorbachev's liberalization to visit their old homeland as American tourists.

The problem of free emigration from the USSR has been a serious obstacle in U.S.–Soviet relations. For an immigrant country such as ours, the very idea of being forbidden to leave one's country is abhorrent. But Russian tradition has always viewed emigration as a sign of disloyalty and ingratitude. Nevertheless, while all those who want to leave the USSR are frowned upon, the fact of Jewish or German emigration is more acceptable. After all, these groups have homelands outside Soviet borders, and the concept of "going back to one's people" makes some sense.

Applicants for emigration take a risk, since until recently the possibility of rejection was great and the repercussions could be unpleasant. In order to get an exit visa (without which nobody can leave the USSR), there is a long list of formalities: one must receive an invitation from abroad (for Jews, until recently, it had to come from Israel), signed by close relatives (how close has varied from time to time), as well as a pile of certificates from a variety of sources ranging from the housing administration to the last place of employment, and also a release from one's own parents (even for "children" over fifty!).

Rejection of an exit visa application does not end there. Until recently the would-be emigrant was likely to be dismissed from his job or demoted to a lesser one, expelled from the university, ostracized by cautious acquaintances, and so on. Cases of extended waiting over many years are well known. Foreign officials traveling to Moscow often have lists of "refuseniks" in their briefcases and try to intercede on their behalf. Improvement of relations with the West, and especially with the United States, leads to a lowering of emigration barriers and to piecemeal releases of old refuseniks. This is a strange phenomenon, as if Moscow were punishing its own citizens for the offenses of foreign powers.

Official Soviet justifications for restrictive emigration policies result in the following self-contradictory arguments:

• It is our own business, a matter of internal policy of our country, and nobody has a right to question it;

• Everybody who so desires has already left and there are no more applications pending;

• Some countries control immigration, the Soviet Union controls emigration. What's wrong with that?

The fact that each justification contradicts another does not seem to matter.

Soviet newspapers have prominently featured articles describing the hardships encountered by former Soviet citizens who now live in the United States, Germany, or Israel. The rare emigrants who permanently returned to the Soviet Union would be pressed to make public condemnations of the capitalist way of life. Stories about the handful of Americans who have decided to seek "political asylum" in the USSR would be skillfully exploited, without ever mentioning the simple fact that anyone who so desires can freely leave the United States in order to live abroad.

Soviet "political refugees" and "defectors" (that is, those Soviet citizens who make the decision to remain in the West while performing, traveling, or residing there on some mission), have been viewed in a much harsher light than simple emigrants. It is only recently that such celebrities as the dancers Baryshnikov and Nureyev have been allowed to visit their relatives in the Soviet Union. More recent "turncoats," as well as those outspokenly critical of the regime, remain unwelcome.

34

Foreigners

Mistrust of foreigners is very old in Russia. In centuries past this attitude had religious as well as political grounds, for Russia felt herself threatened and surrounded by alien ideas and peoples. Russia's Orthodox coreligionists were under domination by Muslim and Catholic powers. Protestant Sweden blocked Russia's access to the Baltic, nomadic Muslims controlled the southern steppes. Foreign merchants allowed into Muscovy were kept under close surveillance. Jews were kept out.

In the seventeenth century there existed in Moscow something called the "German suburb," a special area within the city where foreigners (at that time mostly German- or Dutch-speaking) were supposed to reside. They lived in better, cleaner, and more secure conditions than the Russians outside the area. They were at once protected from the natives and prevented from "contaminating" them, thanks to close surveillance by the authorities. Tsar Peter the Great, who opened Russia to the West and sent many young Russian nobles to study abroad, was favorable to Western influence. He found the German suburb to his taste and spent a good deal of time there during his youth, but he did not discontinue the surveillance of foreigners.

After the ascension of German-born Catherine the Great, a new element came to dominate the concern about contact with foreigners: the fear of revolutionary, antimonarchist ideas coming from the West, especially France. The rise of Napoleon brought yet another fear: fear of invasion by more powerful and modern western armies. This fear has been reinforced several times—in the Crimean War of 1854, World War I and the War of Intervention, and World War II.

The fledgling Soviet regime born in the chaos of World War I and first tested militarily by Western forces in league with its own internal enemies, early acquired an intolerance and distrust of anything "alien." As revolutionary uprisings one after another failed in other countries, it became clear that the Soviet Union would have to survive in isolation and without allies, the world's sole socialist state. This embattled outlook persisted through the decades.

With the rise of Mikhail Gorbachev and his policies of *glasnost* and *perestroika*, the USSR has embarked upon a great reopening to the world, particularly the West. In many ways this outreach is reminiscent of Peter the Great's quest to invigorate Russia with new technologies and new attitudes, and in some it excites the same concern that these infusions will bring instability and undesirable change. The walls built up over centuries will not be brought down overnight.

Being a foreigner in the USSR today is a unique experience of life in a "gilded cage." To understand what this typically means, a review of official regulations—and some common sense rules of conduct—may be of help. It should be noted that many of the restrictions mentioned here were not being enforced in the late 1980s, or at least not in Moscow and Leningrad.

A Soviet tourist or business visa is not enough to entitle a foreigner to travel across the country or to stay with friends or relatives. For that purpose, a special visa is needed, one that takes much longer to obtain. Moreover, a separate city visa is needed for each destination, and special permits are required to venture outside of city limits, unless one is a participant in an organized excursion for foreigners.

When a visa is secured abroad, the cities to be visited are already listed. Additional ones can be applied for while in the Soviet Union, through Intourist (the Soviet tourist body in charge of foreign visitors) or the host organization. These organizations assume the task of processing the formalities.

Tourists coming to the USSR in their own cars, or traveling in tourist buses, must have their itinerary fixed in advance and reservations booked. No deviations are allowed without special permission.

Foreign tourists or business visitors are assigned rooms in Intourist hotels or motels, while scholars and students may be sent to academic residences. One rarely learns the name of one's hotel in advance. The daily rate charged to foreigners is at least triple that billed to Soviet citizens for the same accommodation. Regular non-Intourist hotels are forbidden to the foreigner, and private renting of rooms (as is done in Poland or Hungary) is not allowed.

Outside accommodations are limited to apartments in the special residential compounds reserved for foreign diplomats, business people, scholars, and other official visitors who bring their families along for an extended stay.

Moscow telephone information refuses to give out the telephone number of a foreign individual or organization, even that of Lufthansa Airline (the latter request was refused under the pretext that it is a "closed-access enterprise"). Soviet citizens who try to get the room number or telephone extension of a foreigner staying in a hotel face similar difficulties.

Within Intourist hotels, access is controlled both at the entrance and at each floor. Visitors are required to secure entrance permits from the special offices set up in each hotel housing foreign guests. Access to foreign residential compounds or offices is guarded by security men, who check the documents of visitors. True, not everything is always strictly enforced. The Soviet visitor's dress and demeanor, as well as the doorman's diligence, play their role (in a hotel, a timely tip can also be of help).

Private persons lodging a foreigner, even for one night, are supposed to report "the event" to police authorities. The average Soviet citizen would rather violate that rule or simply shy from offering his hospitality: reporting an overnight visit might lead to unnecessary complications. Driving out of town with a foreigner in one's car is even more risky. The road police (GAI) stop cars at their discretion, and having an unauthorized foreign passenger on board is not advisable.

Many institutions and enterprises which by their nature are bound to have visitors from abroad used to compile "lists of persons allowed to deal with foreigners." While there are no lists of persons prohibited from dealing with foreigners (except for Soviet citizens in security-sensitive work), "unauthorized" socializing with them remains highly suspicious.

Thus a foreigner's Soviet friends might prefer if he calls from a telephone booth, instead of the hotel room. They would rather drop him off at a distance from his hotel. They will ask him to keep silent while in the corridors of their apartment building, in order not to attract undue attention. The degree of caution exercised by Soviet citizens varies, with several factors entering into consideration. As a rule, older people traumatized during Stalin's era, those in high positions with a lot to lose, and those more timid by nature, are the most cautious. Younger persons, as well as those in low-paying jobs or in the liberal professions, are more daring.

Soviet scholars, experts, and technicians whose contact is sought by their foreign counterparts do not feel free to respond on their own, or even to receive foreign visitors in their offices, without prior authorization coming from the "foreign relations" departments of their home institutions. A few Soviet professionals are in a position to overlook such restrictions, but the majority are not.

For the average citizen, to socialize with a foreigner beyond a single unplanned meeting still presents some risk. It is a risk not of being arrested, as was the case in Stalin's time, but of possible obstacles to promotion or travel abroad; at the least there may be "discussion" about the "incident." After all, questions about "relatives abroad" are still part of the routine "autobiographies" required of all job seekers. A report about an "incident"

Voices

"For about four years I worked as a translator in the Trade Office in Kransnodar in the field of technical equipment installation. Different [foreigners] came through, but I only established good, friendly relations with a few. . . .

One of the specialists from the Federal Republic of Germany, with whom our family corresponded a long time, was passing through Krasnodar going to Novorossiisk. He cabled me about it and asked me to meet him. He wanted to give me a gift for the new baby . . . something knitted by his wife. . . . The specialist asked Z., who was escorting him, for permission to drop by our place . . . to congratulate my wife personally, give her his family's gifts, and take a picture. From the beginning to the end of the visit, Z. was present; and he right away took down the data from my passport, although he'd known me for three years. . . .

On May 8 I was called to the militia station, where an OVIR [immigration] official, K., in the presence of the deputy director of the Krasnodar OVIR (whose name I cannot recall) had a "talk" with me concerning violations of laws and the harm from friendly contacts with foreigners, especially those from capitalist countries. . . .

'We are giving you a warning this first time,' they told me in conclusion. 'You have no right to meet foreigners outside of working hours. We will learn if somebody visits you again. The second time—a fine of up to fifty rubles.' And more threats were thrown at me about my future.

This is how I was made into an internal enemy of my country.

The head of the Trade Office prohibited anyone giving me even written assignments. Some acquaintances began to avoid me. How can one explain my case in view of our own appeals for trust and cooperation internationally?"

From a letter to *Ogonek*, November 1987

with a foreigner may be filed somewhere, either at work, at the party cell, or with the police, thus paving the way to potential problems should some unforeseen complications arise. Even under *glasnost*, the fear of dealing with foreigners has not fully subsided, at least not yet.

A relationship with someone of the opposite sex, when one partner is Soviet and the other is a foreigner, is even more complicated than professional and social contacts. To start with, motives are suspect from the very outset. Is the Soviet partner really interested in one's company or just looking for short-supply goods the foreigner can provide? Or worse, is the interest police-inspired (not frequent, but still a possible occurrence)?

In this state of affairs only two kinds of relationships can flourish: accidental brief encounters or serious affairs. Anything in between can always trigger the question: is the whole thing worth the trouble of overcoming obstacles and doubts?

If the relationship becomes serious and leads to marriage, a new set of problems arises. During the postwar years, marriage between Soviet and foreign citizens was legally prohibited. Legal obstacles were dropped a long time ago, but an air of official uneasiness remains. Although in the majority of cases the Soviet partner is allowed to leave the country, bureaucratic formalities are endless, and in some unlucky cases the procedure has dragged on for years. Reams of paperwork, appeals to higher authorities, and long-term separation are not very encouraging prospects. Soviet spouses of foreigners are often subjected to humiliating lectures by all kinds of local officials right after the joyous wedding ceremony.

In addition to the obstacles to personal contacts, there are communication difficulties between the USSR and the "capitalist countries." The mail to and from the Soviet Union is very slow: a letter takes weeks to reach its destination. Foreign mail can be subjected to control, making people less willing to write. In the past "corresponding with abroad" was treated as an offense.

Housewives, older people, or those who are known to have relatives abroad are more willing to write and receive letters, but people who have career aspirations may be hesitant to correspond.

The postage for a letter to a capitalist country costs fifty kopeks, or ten times the cost of a local letter, as against only a twofold difference between foreign and domestic mail in the United States. The same goes for telephone calls. A minute of conversation from the USSR to Western Europe costs three rubles per minute, to the United States six rubles. There is a minimum charge of three minutes. This is ten times the cost of a long-distance intercity call; in the United States the comparison would be only 1:2. This "supertax" on international communication cannot possibly be explained in terms of real costs. Rather, it has served to discourage contacts between Soviet citizens and "capitalist" foreigners. The fact that calls and letters from the USSR to Eastern Europe are in line with Soviet internal tariffs confirms that judgment.

Books, journals, and newspapers mailed from abroad are censored, and "undesirable" ones may not be delivered at all. They may be diverted instead to certain Soviet libraries serving as depositories for "special collections" of "dangerous books." Thus foreign books covering subjects deemed controversial rarely reach their destination. Mailing printed matter from the USSR is a problem as well: anything printed before 1975 requires a special permit. Moreover, books to be mailed have to be brought unpacked to the post office, for easier inspection.

Mailing clothing to the USSR is no less of a problem. Despite an acute demand for scarce European or American goods, until recently heavy entrance duties were collected on each item. Secondhand goods were not allowed in, a policy clearly aimed at curtailing the inflow of gifts from friends and relatives, and consequently limiting personal relations and the maintenance of family ties.

Since human and professional contacts are restricted by a

Voices

"Those foreign books and newspapers that are received by our libraries reside mostly in special collections. In order to get access to such a collection, you have to receive a special pass, signed and certified by a scholarly institution and by the library itself. In that permit the theme of the research must be formulated (in order to avoid, God forbid, that a physicist reads something in philosophy, or a philosopher in physics). Why this piling up of permits? Anyhow, without a passport and a diploma one cannot register oneself in an academic library. Why are documents proving citizenship and educational level not enough to give access to all the information available in the library? Where does this psychosis of mistrust come from?

Look in the alphabetical catalogue of foreign publications: out of thirty titles, between seven and nine bear the fateful number '15' and are kept in special collections.

Partisans of 'special' and 'secret' [classifications] in the field of information have an old argument: the ideological 'health' of the nation. One likes to remind those people of an elementary physiological principle: health should not be guarded but supported, and not in hothouses but in the open air."

From a letter to *Ogonek*, November 1987

whole array of measures, foreigners visiting the USSR often feel somehow uncomfortable, even though they enjoy numerous advantages granted by the authorities. These include the use of special waiting lounges at major airports, priority in boarding an airliner, a good chance of bypassing a restaurant queue, easier access to museums, priority reservations in resort areas, and so forth. What is more important, foreign currency opens the door to special hard-currency stores, restaurants, and bars, where short-supply items are readily available, though never for rubles.

Today, Intourist hotels and specially assigned housing compounds for foreigners do not form a separate geographic area within the city limits, but they possess the same gilded-cage aspect. They house foreigners who are supposed to be protected and pampered on one hand, but watched over and kept from fraternizing with the natives on the other. All this creates strange surroundings for the partly ostracized, partly privileged foreign visitor.

Officially, Soviet authorities favor contacts between their own citizens and foreigners. But our view of what such contacts are supposed to be is drastically different from that traditionally held by the Soviet bureaucracy. We tend to think of human contact as a one-to-one affair, an opportunity to make friends, to be invited to someone's home, to discuss in private any possible subject of shared interest, to enjoy a romance if such is the mutual desire. Among themselves, Soviet citizens follow exactly the same pattern. But in dealing with foreigners, the official preference has been for limited encounters under strict supervision with preselected partners. Tourists are supposed to visit sights and not people, at least not in private, students are to socialize with Communist Youth officials, visiting foreign scholars are to be channeled to officially sponsored interviews, and foreign businessmen are directed after working hours to hard-currency bars and restaurants, where better food and service is available and natives are excluded.

Fortunately, official restrictions are not always strictly followed, and nowadays they are readily ignored. An energetic visitor eventually manages to see more than he or she was supposed to, and even to make friends and develop some genuine feeling for the country. But the burden of the past and the uncertainty of the future still hamper the development of steady, continuous relationships between Soviet and foreign citizens. This state of affairs has improved a great deal under Gorbachev, but there is still a long way to go.

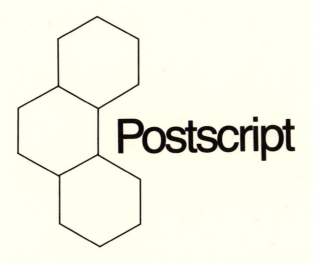

Postscript

35

Perestroika or Nedostroika?

Americans tend to see Mikhail Gorbachev's policy of *perestroika* (restructuring) of the Soviet system as a genuine attempt to bring badly needed changes, an attempt that faces both serious obstacles and strong opposition, especially from the entrenched bureaucracy. But beyond that point, our grasp of what is happening in the Soviet Union today is fairly limited.

The most common mistake is to assume that reform is a popular cause and to view the Soviet bureaucracy as the sole opponent of change. Resistance to *perestroika* comes from other quarters as well. Workers, for example, are being asked to perform better for more pay. But they are accustomed to taking a slapdash approach to work, where their main obligation was to meet quantitative production quotas, no more and no less. Promised financial incentives are not much of an inducement for hard work if consumer goods (including, of course, vodka) are not readily available at any price. Other concerns are that workers' job security is threatened by the prospect of layoffs in the interest of efficiency, or that the energy needed for after-hours moonlighting might be exhausted on the job. A widespread worry is that a comprehensive price reform (something that is much needed) will deprive consumers of the low-priced staples and basic services they have long regarded as their entitlement.

The role of the growing Soviet middle class as a driving force behind the reforms is the most overlooked factor. The middle class extends well beyond the intelligentsia and includes such varied elements as skilled workers, trade and service personnel, members of liberal professions, and generally "solid citizens." While they too may be threatened with the loss of job security, they tend to be confident of their ability to fend for themselves in a more open economy, especially when personal initiative is increasingly encouraged and it is clear that people's skills need to be put to better uses.

This is the social group that stands behind the Gorbachev reforms. It shares universal middle-class values, taking basic material well-being, social responsibility, a dose of self-reliance, and access to goods and services for granted. It puts a high value on *glasnost* (openness) and the reinvigoration of Soviet cultural life that Gorbachev has fostered. The lower classes, by and large, have not attained the levels of material and social security that underpin these middle-class attitudes. At the other end of the social spectrum, those who have made their careers in the "command and control" system, supervising the implementation of central directives and preventing the exercise of initiative of any kind, have an obvious stake in the preservation of the old system.

A general inertia, combined with long-ingrained habits, presents another serious obstacle to reform. People are being asked to change their work habits, show initiative, pay attention to quality, and accept even wider financial disparities—all within a short time, and with no immediate reward. Of course, as in any time of economic change, enterprising spirits, including not a few profiteers and opportunists, have been quick to surface. But, not surprisingly, the majority of people remain cautious and continue to do things the old familiar way, while paying lip service to the necessity of change. This is all the more true since practical results from the reforms—such as improvements in food supplies—have yet to be seen.

The failure of the kolkhoz system is common knowledge, but this key institution in the Soviet system has long been regarded as untouchable. Gorbachev initially proposed only modest reforms in agriculture, most notably the family contract, a sort of "sharecropping" arrangement under the aegis of the kolkhoz. Now, with the food supply situation approaching crisis, he has proposed a ''radical restructuring'' of the farm system and a ''New Agrarian Policy'' that will effect a transition to leasehold farming and a free market in agricultural products. It is too soon to predict the fate of these proposals, but their urgency is beyond question.

Shifting state enterprises to genuine cost accounting and requiring them to operate profitably is another important reform only imperfectly realized in the Gorbachev program. While managers are being exhorted both to produce more efficiently and to run their plants more democratically, the fact is that the enterprises remain tied to the government ministries and that their top priority is still the fulfillment of state orders. Under these circumstances, enterprise autonomy is a fiction, and to expect that plants will begin to function more flexibly and efficiently is not very realistic.

Another area where the reform program has been weakened by ambivalence and inconsistency is in legalizing existing private ''businesses'' and encouraging the opening of new, more productive ones. The private sector as it is being conceived, with its tiny cooperatives, limited private services, and marginal operations, remains largely outside the the general economic system. It is mostly confined to the traditional services, formerly available on the ''gray market'' but recently legalized, yet hemmed in with regulations, restrictions, and prohibitive income taxes. A genuine ''mixed economy,'' with a private sector encompassing a substantial share of economic activity, is not yet envisioned. As long as this is the case, the public sector, inefficient in many domains, will not face the sort of genuine competition that would force it either to improve or to withdraw from those fields where its performance is weakest.

Perhaps the most important problem calling for reform is the duplicate system of command and control, with the party apparatus paralleling and overseeing the government administrative bureaucracy in every area. In theory, government officials administer and party officials control. In reality, the party meddles in everything, details included, reducing the state bureaucracy to order-taking with little initiative of its own.

The problem is even more acute in the republics and other administrative subunits, where, in addition to the usual duplications, federal interference in even the most trivial matters paralyzes local initiative and offends national sensitivities.

This system not only inflates the size of the bureaucracy but slows down every possible endeavor. Unless the party leaves day-to-day operations to governmental agencies, withdraws from routine economic management, and concentrates on purely political and ideological matters, the efficiency of the present system cannot possibly be improved. But the outlook for the reforms in this area is most difficult to gauge.

Thus, without overhauling the kolkhoz system, without allowing enterprises to function as autonomous economic units, without accepting the principle of a genuinely mixed competitive economy (even if predominantly state-controlled), without removing the party from routine administrative and economic affairs, and without allowing the republics much more leeway in handling local and regional problems, the current restructuring will not succeed. If Gorbachev fails to remove those obstacles from the path of his reforms, the result will be *nedostroika* (unfinished construction), not *perestroika*.

For Further Reading

Friedberg, Maurice, and Heyward Isham, eds., *Soviet Society Under Gorbachev: Current Trends and the Prospects for Reform* (Armonk: M. E. Sharpe, 1987).

Heller, Mikhail, and Alexander M. Nekrich, *Utopia in Power: The History of the Soviet Union from 1917 to the Present* (New York, Summit Books, 1986).

Kerblay, Basile, *Modern Soviet Soviety* (New York: Pantheon Books, 1983).

Lewin, Moshe, *The Gorbachev Phenomenon* (Berkeley: University of California Press, 1988).

McClellan, Woodford, *Russia: A History of the Soviet Period* (Englewood Cliffs: Prentice Hall, 1985).

Medish, Vadim, *The Soviet Union* (Englewood Cliffs: Prentice Hall, 1987).

Shipler, David, *Russia: Broken Idols, Solemn Dreams* (New York: Times Books, 1983).

Smith, Hedrick, *The Russians* (New York: Times Books, 1977).

Voslensky, Michael, *Nomenklatura: The Soviet Ruling Class* (Garden City: Doubleday, 1984).

Index

About the Author

Michael Rywkin, born in eastern Poland, spent his youth in France and in the USSR. He attended higher educational institutions in Samarkand, Lodz, Paris, and New York where he completed a doctorate in political science at Columbia University. During his most recent trips to the Soviet Union on the U.S.-USSR academic exchange, in 1984 and 1987, he visited the cities of Baku, Bukhara, Erevan, Khiva, Leningrad, Moscow, Samarkand, Tallin, Tartu, Tashkent, and Tbilisi.

Currently professor of Russian Area Studies at the City College of the City University of New York, Rywkin is also chairman of the Association for the Study of Nationalities (USSR and Eastern Europe). He is the author of *Moscow's Muslim Challenge: Soviet Central Asia* (also published by M. E. Sharpe, Inc.) and editor of *Russian Colonial Expansion to 1917.*